8-BIT
APOCALYPSE

8-BIT APOCALYPSE

THE UNTOLD STORY OF ATARI'S *MISSILE COMMAND*

ALEX RUBENS

WITH A FOREWORD BY JEFF GERSTMANN

THE OVERLOOK PRESS
NEW YORK

This edition first published in hardcover in the United States in 2018 by
The Overlook Press, Peter Mayer Publishers, Inc.

NEW YORK
141 Wooster Street
New York, NY 10012
www.overlookpress.com
For bulk and special sales, please contact sales@overlookny.com
or write to us at the above address.

Cataloging-in-Publication Data is available from the Library of Congress
A catalog record for this book is available from the British Library

Book design and typeformatting by Bernard Schleifer
Manufactured in the United States of America
FIRST EDITION
1 3 5 7 9 10 8 6 4 2
ISBN 978-1-4683-1644-5

For my wife, Sydnee.

In nuclear war, all men are cremated equal.
—DEXTER GORDON

Contents

Foreword

W HEN IT COMES TO EARLY GAME DEVELOPMENT, YOU HEAR A couple of different stories over and over again. Either it was an incredibly serious crew of people busting out some masterpiece of programming in their garage or it was driven by bong rips and hot tubs. Actually, sometimes it seems like most video games of the late 1970s and early 1980s are the result of a bit of both. That's what makes Dave Theurer's story so significant. The development of *Missile Command* was decidedly different than the other games of its era. It's the first example of a game's concept being "ripped from the headlines," deliberately conceived to reflect the low-key panic of the Cold War in ways that, these days, might seem a little crude. But upon reading Alex's reporting here and trying to put myself in the shoes of Theurer as he attempts to create what might be the very first video game with a message, it's easy to see just how overwhelming this process could be.

Of course, I didn't receive any part of Theurer's message at first. I was five when *Missile Command* was completed and sent off to arcades, and the main message I received was "you are too young to handle a game with this high-precision trackball and three separate fire buttons." I mostly stared at the cabinet as other people played because the flashing, cycling explosions that mark a player's demise were some of the coolest-looking things in video games back then. Then I'd go off to play *Galaxian* or shake my head at the massive line of people waiting for their chance to play *Pac-Man*.

I connected with *Missile Command* when it came home. My parents, thinking that computers might be good for education, picked up an Atari 400 and before long, I had a home version of *Missile Command* at the ready. Here, the trackball was replaced by a standard joystick, and instead of having to deal with three separate missile bases, there was only one base and one fire button. I got pretty good, but it never really translated into any real skill at the arcade version.

Over the years, *Missile Command* remained a respected arcade game. A lot of games started getting remade or "remastered" in newer ways. A few attempts were made at making "new" versions of *Missile Command*, but they were universally lame. Attempts to reissue the original game were usually hamstrung by the lack of a good trackball-style control option, making it harder to appreciate these days. Also, the timing was all wrong. We were in a different era, and remakes released in a time where thoughts of nuclear destruction were firmly on the back burner could never resonate the way the game did in 1980. In the twenty-three years I've spent covering games, the ones that attempted to re-create the gameplay of *Missile Command* never got it right. As a result, *Missile Command* didn't benefit from our long nostalgia boom the way franchises like *Donkey Kong* or *Pac-Man* have. It faded into the background as a classic that modern players wouldn't really have a chance to connect with. I never spent much time thinking about it until the day a *Missile Command* arcade cabinet showed up on my doorstep. Someone was actually trying to throw it away, and we were able to rescue it just before it found its way into a landfill for good.

Of course, the cabinet didn't actually work.

I'm no electronics wizard, but I can certainly blow dust,

gunk, and spiders out of the inside of an arcade machine. After a thorough wipe down and some time spent carefully tapping the ROMs in the hopes that they just needed to be reseated into the PCB a bit, I lucked out. The machine fired up. Sure, the speakers were blown out and the monitor wasn't emitting an especially clean signal, but it was still playable. Adding to the overall appeal of having one in my home is that it also happens to be a uniquely beautiful cabinet. The side art has a chunky, colorful style to it that evokes the era quite well. It's also slightly shorter than a lot of other cabinets from the old days, which is something you'll learn more about later on in the book. My *Missile Command* cabinet still needs some work, but even with a monitor that desperately needs servicing and blown-out speakers, *Missile Command*'s colorful graphics and fast action are bright enough to blast through nearly forty years of dust and decay. It's a fantastic cabinet. I'm also happy to report I've finally gained enough dexterity to handle all three missile bases at the same time without panicking.

I'm also old enough now to see what Theurer was going for, and a how a game that might seem so abstract by today's standards could haunt a person so thoroughly during its development. With today's political climate bringing back some of those Cold War feelings from the bad old days and an increasing focus on labor issues and the "crunch culture" that is burning out some of modern game development's brightest minds, Alex has chosen a fascinating time to look back at a game that dealt with those issues nearly forty years ago. I hope you get at least as much out of this look back at those early days as I did.

—Jeff Gerstmann
04/23/2018

Introduction

ISSILE COMMAND IS JUST ONE OF *THOSE* GAMES. THE GAMES that you may have never played, but could describe perfectly because of how often you've seen it. The games that stick out as something so unique and different, there's been very little that could ever compare. The games that, in spite of all odds, you can't shake from your memory, even decades after your last play.

The game is many different things to many different people, but for me, it's always been one of the few games that have been able to stand the test of time and transcend generations. It doesn't matter if you're five or fifty, you can play *Missile Command* and find enjoyment in it.

I still remember my time with the game fondly, asking for quarters and sneaking in a few games every time my family went for pizza. The pizza wasn't very good, but it was *our spot*, and it had games; that trade-off was always worth it. I was terrible at the game, failing to grasp how the trackball worked at such a young age, but that didn't stop me from trying. Besides, all the other games were lame, especially to play by yourself.

There wasn't anything like *Missile Command*. It was fast and exciting, pushing me to improve not only as my understanding of the game developed but also as my body became more attuned to the fine motor skills required to play the game at a high level. It required the utmost precision, and that wasn't something I was really able to handle at such a young age. I wasn't in it for the top score. I just wanted to have fun, and *Missile Command* was perfect for that. It was beautiful and captivating, in a package that couldn't be replicated anywhere else.

As I grew up, so did my pizza parlor's arcade. New games were welcomed in and old games were quietly shuffled out, like Andy's toys in the movie *Toy Story*, either because they were perpetually down for maintenance or they just weren't drawing the quarters they once were. Whatever the cause, the arcade became more of a money-grabbing pit to pull kids away from their quarters than an experience centering on fun and exploration. Then, just like that, *Missile Command* was gone, never to be enjoyed by pizza-awaiting kids again.

At the same time, I, along with many others, began to make the transition away from arcades and toward home consoles. I had my Nintendo Entertainment System and Nintendo 64, and I could play games whenever I wanted; I didn't need to wait for it to be pizza night. As I continued down this path, arcades became a thing of the past. We would venture out for friends' birthday parties, or a fun family outing, but going to the arcade wasn't a regular occurrence anymore. *Missile Command* came and went from my thoughts, fading into the background as new and more modern games took hold of my attention. And yet, even as time passed, the game never fully left. Its place as a staple of pop culture, bolstered by nostalgia for the Atari age, was a constant reminder of something that had captivated me so long ago.

Then, in 2012, I stumbled on a story that would bring the game back to the forefront of my thoughts, quickly consuming my every action as I set off to discover more about the story of one man who had brought joy—and dread—to so many gamers decades earlier.

WE SAT AT the bar of the Marriott in downtown San Francisco, across the street from Moscone Center, where the annual Game Developers Conference (GDC) was happening. I was in town for the conference, but my main goal was an interview I was conducting for my debut story on IGN.com, gaming's biggest news outlet. A few weeks earlier I had attended the premiere of the Smithsonian Institution's exhibit *The Art of Video Games* at MoPOP, the Museum of Pop Culture, in Seattle, where I was living at the time, and needed to grab an interview to tie the whole thing together.

It was an amazing exhibit that really captured the spirit of gaming and what made it so special, collecting games from the last few decades and bringing them together for players to learn about their histories and experience them with friends. Chris Melissinos, the exhibit's curator, had received the GDC Ambassador Award earlier in the week for his work on the exhibit, and he agreed to meet with me for the story.

Chris had an energy unlike anyone I had ever interviewed before. It was filled with such deep passion and appreciation for the art of gaming, you couldn't help but become inspired speaking to him. Plenty of other interview subjects had been passionate about the projects they were working on, but you could tell that Chris had this infectious, all-consuming love for gaming that pervaded every word that he spoke.

He wasn't a museum curator by trade. Chris had started working at Sun Microsystems in the mid-1990s as a sales manager, but his love for gaming was uncontrollable. He quickly earned the title of Chief Gaming Officer (however one does that) and became the face of what the company was attempting to do in the industry. His job was essentially to become an evangelist for gaming and convince people they would be regretting it for the rest of their lives if they missed out. After learning this, it's clear where his passion for sharing what makes a game so special came from. But he left that behind, and eventually went to work for Verizon, developing corporate growth strategies—quite a shift from gaming. But he was too passionate not to share the impact of video games with those who he felt needed it most—hence *The Art of Video Games*.

As we sat there, sharing stories back and forth, Chris blew me away with story after story of passionate game development that made the art form so special to him. One of these stories was about Dave Theurer and the creation of *Missile Command*. I was immediately captivated by the story of a man driven by such strong passion for his creation that he pushed too far, becoming consumed by his work and facing haunting visions of the very project he had dedicated himself to. Even the quick, told-at-the-bar version of the story was nothing short of extraordinary.

We had a great talk—one that I truly never wanted to end, because I couldn't believe so many of these stories existed. I wanted to hear them all. As I left, I couldn't get the story of Dave Theurer out of my head, shocked that I'd never heard anything about it in all my years in the industry. I pulled out my smartphone, trying to do some cursory digging, but had trouble finding anything even somewhat related to the topic. There were murmurs here and there, and people had discussed it at one point or another, but for there to be that powerful a story behind such a momentous game as *Missile Command*, I thought it would be a little more publicized. Then I realized why it wasn't: Dave Theurer himself.

There were discussions of this, but never any interviews. He hadn't spoken about it; it was almost as if he had disappeared following the game's release, despite its massive impact on the industry. Without a story, you can't have much of a history. As I investigated further, I found that following his work on *Missile Command*, Theurer had worked on a few other projects before leaving the gaming industry altogether, opting for a more traditional programming job at a major software development company.

For Theurer, this was a much more comfortable environment. Games were too intense, too personal. He devoted too much of himself to them, personalizing the context and making it feel as though he was sharing a bit of what he felt directly with the players, regardless of who they were or how they played the game. It was a tough thing to work through for months on end, especially with the deeply creative subject matter they were exploring at the time. It was the height of the Cold War, and tensions were high. Working at Atari was an escape for most, but filling his every waking hour with nuclear war and monsters didn't really fit with Theurer's definition of fulfilling. He wanted something a bit more comfortable and sustainable, and he didn't want to have to worry about something so haunting, so he left the games industry.

That's when my obsession began to take form. How powerful could these nightmares surrounding one of gaming's most notable titles have been that the creator wanted nothing to do with gaming anymore? And what had caused them? Now, that's a story worth telling.

The only problem was that Atari was now a shell of its former self. It had collapsed nearly two decades earlier as it was sold off for names and licenses alone for less than $5 million, despite its billion-dollar revenues as the fastest growing company in the history of the United States just years earlier.

Theurer's story had happened way back in 1980, and there was no way that anyone who worked at Atari then was still working there now. I had to get creative if I wanted to hear more. Most of the documentation around these projects was thrown out when it was deemed no longer necessary, so looking into that wouldn't be a possibility.

Yet the more bleak it looked, the more determined I was to find out more. With a little searching, I was able to find contact info for those tangentially connected to Theurer, hoping they might be able to steer me in the right direction. I contacted Rob Fulop, who ported *Missile Command* to the Atari 2600, but he didn't have any updated contact information for Theurer. He did, however, reveal to me that Theurer hadn't been the only programmer working on the project, despite that usually being the case at the time. He had a junior programmer assigned to the project with him, Rich Adam, who Fulop could put me in touch with.

Adam told me all about their work on the project, what it was like to work at Atari during that time, and—most important—what it was like to work with Dave Theurer. Adam hadn't encountered any of the same struggles that Theurer had, but he understood why Theurer might have. To Adam, Theurer was an idol, and Adam saw how something as powerful as *Missile Command* could really affect someone, especially in the culture they found themselves in at Atari in the 1980s. Unfortunately, he couldn't help me get in touch with Theurer either—it had been years since they had last spoken, and Adam left Atari long before Theurer, so he didn't have any insight on where he went post-Atari.

Dejected, I tried to find out as much info on Theurer as I could, hoping an opportunity would jump out from the little information available online. Just a year earlier, he had actually been presented with the Pioneer Award at the Game Developers Conference. The award was presented to those "who developed a breakthrough technology, game concept, or gameplay design" and had been given to industry legends like Gabe Newell, founder of Valve Corporation, and Alexey Pajitnov, the creator of *Tetris*. This only added to the mystery of Theurer's story. How could someone who very few have ever heard of be up there with such industry innovators?

I contacted a friend who was able to connect me with the general manager of the GDC to see if there was potential for reaching Theurer. Minutes later, I had a response. As it turned out, they had faced the same difficulties I was facing. Theurer was like a ghost; he wanted nothing to do with the industry and had worked hard to remove himself from it, shifting the focus of his work to a more modest profession.

With much better sleuthing skills than I, they were able to track down his current employer through a patent filing and, in a last-ditch attempt, fired off an email to the generic info@company.com address listed on their website. And they got a response. I followed the same path, hoping to get a similar response and finally be one step closer to hearing about the story that had captivated my every thought for months.

It felt like things were finally starting to come together. I had the email address; who knew if they'd reply, but I was at least on the right track for figuring out how to reach him. I drafted an email, sweating over every detail, hoping they would understand the nature of the request and take pity enough to pass it along to Theurer. I couldn't afford any mistakes; this was my shot.

Finally comfortable with my pitch, I hit Send, immediately getting an eerie feeling that I had just encountered yet another dead end. That night I lay awake in my bed, unable to sleep. Every possible permutation of what Theurer might say swirled around in my head, like a cartoon bowl of alphabet soup.

With the sun rising outside my window, I gave up on my foolish endeavor to sleep and went to get a cup of coffee. When I returned, I sat down at my desk and opened my email to find something new waiting for me: a response from Dave Theurer. My heart raced as I sat frozen, unable to click the mouse hovering over the email subject. My mind couldn't comprehend what I was seeing: he had actually responded.

I opened the email and was treated to the thirteen most disappointing words of my life:

> Hello Alex,
> I don't do interviews anymore due to time constraints.
> Thanks,
> Dave

Straight to the point: it was a no. He wasn't interested in talking to me—and that meant there would be no story. Theurer's legacy would remain a secret kept between him and the game, never to be heard from again. Disappointed, I thanked him and moved on. As a writer, I knew I couldn't spend any more time on this. Deadlines were short, and editors didn't have patience for writers chasing down stories that people weren't interested in telling. I went on to tell other stories—stories that, had I not heard the premise of Theurer's, would have been exceptionally compelling. But since I had, they felt like nothing more than second-class amalgams of the same narrative that had been told time and time again.

I had to give it another shot, even if it meant speaking to everyone in the world *but* Dave Theurer. I followed up on every other lead I could possibly chase, talking to anyone who had anything to do with Atari or *Missile Command* during his tenure. I was getting good stuff and learning a lot about the eventual outcome, but it was missing the *why*. It was a beautiful picture, but was lacking the journey of how they had gotten there. It didn't feel complete. It needed Theurer.

In a last-ditch effort before abandoning the project forever, I sent one final email.

> Hi Dave,
> I wanted to get in touch with you one last time to let you know that I spoke with other members of the *Missile*

Command dev[elopment] team on the experience of developing the game and they brought up some things that I would love your opinion on.

If you can find the time to speak with me for even twenty minutes, I would really appreciate it.

Alex

Days passed, and my already low expectations began to fall to unforeseen depths. Just as I thought it was time to give it up, as if he could sense my defeated desperation through the email, Theurer responded. Anticipating another rejection, I let the email sit unopened for a whole day. I'd become so dedicated to the project that I was worried I'd let the rejection determine the project's significance, and I didn't want that. Eventually coming to terms with what was likely contained inside, I opened the email.

Much to my surprise, Theurer agreed to an interview.

I couldn't believe it: he was willing to talk to me, and I was going to be able to tell the impossible story. Over the course of the next few months, Theurer and I exchanged emails and spent hours on the phone discussing his time at Atari, his work on both *Missile Command* and *Tempest*, and—most important— his fears with participating in such a story for the industry that had brought him so much sorrow decades earlier.

What follows is the unbelievable journey through the tumultuous creation of one of gaming's most iconic arcade classics as recounted by those who lived through it.

This is the story of *Missile Command* and the heroic man who made it a reality.

8-BIT
APOCALYPSE

At Any Moment

1

THOUGH WE MAY LOOK BACK ON AND REMEMBER THE 1980s as an action-packed neon factory where Bruce Willis, Arnold Schwarzenegger, arcades, and workout videos reigned supreme, it wasn't always like that, especially at the beginning of the decade. We weren't yet talking about Michael Jordan's famous series-winning basket, "The Shot," or dancing along to Michael Jackson's *Thriller*. This all came down the road, but those final years of the late 1970s and early 1980s were a much different time, filled with haunting, unending fear.

With the dwindling economy set in motion by the administration of President Jimmy Carter, tough economic times were causing people to approach their daily lives in a different manner from how they had in the 1960s. It wasn't as easy to get a well-paying job, or any job at all. Unemployment was on the rise (and would continue to climb, reaching the highest point in United States history in 1983), making it more difficult for Americans to support their families and build any kind of safety net. If you were able to find a job, you most likely weren't focused on building a career that was personally fulfilling and focusing on your personal passions. A lot of people were just barely scraping by. It was extremely apparent at the time, permeating the national consciousness. Unease loomed over daily life like a storm cloud that could start spitting out lightning at any moment.

There wasn't certainty in any sector, and personal and national security least of all. It wasn't a time to take risks or venture outside your comfort zone. Many were struggling just to survive through another day, but little did they know there was a much larger threat looming above.

The Cold War had been going on for decades, starting just after World War II ended in 1945, and had turned from a specific event into a perpetual state of being. Though Germany had been defeated by the Allied powers, the Soviet Union didn't want to relinquish power so easily. Instead, it gave the appearance of being peaceful, but was slowly consolidating all of the Eastern Bloc countries under its reign following along the protocol of the Molotov–Ribbentrop Pact, which the USSR and Nazi Germany had signed in 1939 as an agreement of nonaggression toward each other during World War II. With two superpowers so close to each other during such a volatile invasion as that being executed by Nazi Germany, it was necessary for the Nazis to have the Soviet Union on their side. Contained within this pact was a secret agreement to divide six countries (Estonia, Finland, Latvia, Lithuania, Poland, and Romania) between them into occupied territories following the invasion of Poland in 1939, establishing new borders and creating what we would later call the Eastern Bloc. Though many of these states weren't officially overthrown during this time, they were considered to be satellite states under Soviet control.

Despite the Soviet Union pulling out of Molotov-Ribbentrop Pact and declaring it void in 1941 following Adolf Hitler's order to attack Soviet strongholds within Eastern Poland, it did not return these countries to independent control and forced them to adopt the Soviet socialist systems, even rigging elections to ensure Soviet ideals would take hold. From the outside, this looked as if the USSR had been acting alone during the war, as the pact's existence wasn't officially confirmed until long after the end of the Cold War in 1989.

Considering that the USSR was an Allied force, this didn't sit well with many countries—especially the United States, which felt the continued occupied invasions were an unnecessary grasp of power. While the US didn't want to start another war following one of the deadliest wars in the history of the world, especially with an official ally, it couldn't let the Soviet Union get away with slowly consolidating more and more countries under its power through hostile means. To counteract this, the US initiated a secret countereffort, funding and supporting all Western European countries who could provide opposition to the encroaching Eastern Bloc and also funding the Manhattan Project, the nuclear research effort that funded what would eventually become the US contribution to the nuclear arms race. Meanwhile, the USSR continued to push more funds into its newly acquired countries and pushed forward with nuclear research of its own. This series of nuclear armament from both the US (and its NATO allies) and the USSR resulted in a secretive and uncomfortable tension between the two nations that only escalated the longer it went on without a resolution.

Yet neither wanted to break protocol, and continued pushing their agendas in the dark, creating what would eventually become the Cold War. With each always concerned about what the other might be doing, both nations (and their allies) continued to push nuclear technology research out of fear it might need to be put into action. This went on for decades, resulting in the largest accumulation of nuclear weapons in history, unsurpassed even to this day. For context, the United States alone ran 1,054 nuclear explosion tests in the period between 1945 and 1992.

This stalemate resulted in one of the largest standoffs in

military history and—despite attempted nuclear reform by the United Nations, which had been formed at the end of the war in 1945—left both nations in a constant state of fear that nuclear war could break out any moment.

While both programs were top secret, it was clear to everyone that this was occurring; even in the best of economic conditions, and had everything else been perfect, the situation would have left most in a perpetual state of uncertainty and fear. And it did just that; there was a feeling of deep-rooted uncertainty. If you start with the fear that you may not be able to support your family and that you'll be kicked out on the street and forced to do anything you can to feed your kids, yet you might just barely succeed; add to that the sight of missiles streaking in from above and the knowledge that everything you know and love could be wiped out in an instant. That state of mind does something to you, and it certainly did for the average American trying to make it through daily life at the time.

——This feeling of discomfort was unshakable, even as the economy began to recover in the mid-1980s. For most, the recovery was a false comfort; how long would it last before it all crumbled again? Could one actually loosen up the purse strings, or would it all fall apart with the next downturn in the stock market? These were the questions plaguing the American psyche at the time.

For some, this meant a shift back to the very same conditions that had haunted them in the previous decade: finally finding jobs and being able to support their families in a more sustainable way, only to begin to worry about losing it once again. For a select few, it was a complete reversal into excess as the stock market exploded in the late 1980s. Bankers and traders on Wall Street, who began making huge deals as the market rose and watched their salaries rise in kind, found themselves experiencing a kind of excess that most Americans couldn't even fathom.

Even as Americans settled into relative economic comfort, a fear still remained—and would throughout the majority of the decade until December 3, 1989, when the Cold War officially ended. But before that point, there were nearly two decades of uncertainty around basic survival, financial stability, and, most of all, the threat of nuclear bombs that could wipe out the entire nation at any moment.

It was years before we'd hit the worst of it in 1983, and early on, things were relatively quiet. Despite the nuclear arms race brewing between the two superpowers for the past thirty years, we hadn't actually heard anything from the USSR in a while. For some, it was a good sign that we weren't getting daily threats to our safety; for others, it was infinitely worse to hear nothing. The silence was deafening, and let fear of the unknown creep into the everyday consciousness in an unsettlingly deep way.

Red Dawn, the film by John Milius, wouldn't come out until 1984, but it perfectly captured the fears of everyday Americans, who were worried that one day they might turn to the sky to see a full-on invasion from the USSR. In the film, two brothers find their small Colorado town invaded by the Soviets, and they're forced to band together to defend it, eventually defeating the opposing forces. The film perfectly encapsulated the fears that people were experiencing at the time, striking a cord in the national consciousness.

The Soviet Union was chosen as the invading force because, at the time, the CIA believed the USSR and Cuba to be the largest threats to national safety.

Though the film may have been a bit over the top in its portrayal, such a scenario was a real fear at the time. There was always concern that the Soviets might hit major cities with their ever-growing nuclear arsenal and then invade what parts of the United States remained. One day you might be trying to figure out how much money to set aside for your future, and the next you could be trading what few rounds of ammunition you had left to ensure that your family could eat for another day until help arrived. This was the potential reality.

This type of primal fear for safety messes with people. You lose sleep; you're always anxious. Paranoia sets in as you wonder if that moment might come where everything you've worked for could blow away in a wave of nuclear heat. In this heightened state, your brain and body are affected in subconscious ways. Fear seeps into your everyday life. Your slightly elevated heart rate, the shakes that you attribute to too much coffee or skipping breakfast—even when you aren't thinking about it, your body and overall state of being are still affected by a general sense of uneasiness that something is coming, yet you have no idea what it is or how to prepare for it.

Worst of all, that fear stuck around. The Cold War lasted nearly forty-five years, and it worked to cement fear as constant and unending. It became a part of life, one that never seemed to subside. In an oddly morbid sense, there was comfort in knowing that everyone else was experiencing the same fears. They might be better at handling it, or might have had fewer other things to worry about, but still they were right there with you; they got it.

As the economy started to pull together, most were starting to regain their sense of safety; immediate survival wasn't as much of a concern, but fear of the unknown lingered: it might not be wise to spend that money on vacation, because if we go to war and we lose our primary source of income due to the draft, we'll be stuck. On the other hand, screw it; we'll all be dead soon enough anyway. All future plans hinged on the ability of a few politicians in Washington, DC, to defuse the long-standing, escalating conflict. This reliance on Washington led to an obsession with information, with everyone trying to stay as updated as possible.

In this quest for constant knowledge, up-and-coming media mogul Ted Turner saw opportunity. He sold off the local news station he owned in North Carolina, WRET, and in 1980, with outside investment from Reese Schonfeld, started CNN, the world's first twenty-four-hour news network, in Atlanta. For the first time ever, you didn't need to wait until ten or eleven o'clock at night to catch the news, hoping nothing important happened later that night. With no publicly available internet at the time, and newspapers that were only printed once or twice a day, any news that broke after those nightly broadcasts would have to wait until the following morning. There was a delay that you just had to deal with if you wanted to get the news; perhaps you'd hear something on the radio if you were driving late enough, but for most, television broadcasts were their primary source of information.

In a nuclear climate where entire countries could potentially be wiped out in an instant, this was less than ideal. Ted Turner saw an opportunity to fill this news void and created CNN, which brought a constant flow of information and access to more world news that ever before. No longer did you need to wait for the story about the local fair to wrap up to find out what was important. While for some it was a relief to be better informed, for others it was a negative experience, as they became locked in a trance, unable to stop watching the unending onslaught of information coming to them at breakneck speed.

This resulted in an odd combination of feeling simultaneously under- and overinformed. People were consuming information at a rate never experienced before, but it didn't feel like it served to keep them more informed about the issues they knew very little about before; rather, it brought to light even more events that they had had no clue were even occurring. The more they watched, the less anyone felt like they really knew the whole story; they knew about an increasing number of news events, but less about each individual event, and more unrelated information snuck its way in.

New revelations about a program happening in the USSR? It was less, "Well, at least we know," and more, "How did we not know about this before?" What was intended as a way to stay informed and quell any fears people may have had instead amplified those fears, increasing the internal anxiety plaguing the American consciousness.

This, of course, is the tenet on which news media is based. If you were to just come for the story you wanted to know about and left, that wouldn't do them much good. But if you got caught up in a few other stories while waiting for the story you're actually interested in, there's a good chance you'll stick around to finish the broadcast now that you're hooked. Ted Turner said it best: "We won't be signing off until the world ends. We'll be on, and we will cover the end of the world, live, and that will be our last event. . . . [A]nd when the end of the world comes, we'll play 'Nearer, My God, to Thee' before we sign off."

With the economy in such dire straits, many found themselves unable to afford to go out to restaurants, enjoy a movie at the local theater, or catch a Van Halen concert, so instead they turned to CNN. It was free (if you had cable TV), and the stories were structured in an entertaining way. It certainly wasn't a replacement for going out, but there was always something happening, and it was right there in your living room. There was a huge draw to this endless source of information, available anytime.

With every new story, it was clear we were living in different times. While the United States was concentrating on expanding the technology of its military and nuclear programs, the Soviet Union was employing traditional espionage tactics, and we never saw it coming. Espionage gave the USSR massive insight into what we were working on at the time. Back at the Potsdam Conference on July 24, 1945, there had been a meeting between Joseph Stalin, the leader of the Soviet Union, US president Harry S. Truman, and UK prime minister Winston Churchill as they met to discuss how to handle the conditions of Nazi Germany's surrender, which had occurred only weeks before. During this meeting Truman famously mentioned to Stalin that the United States "had a new weapon of unusual destructive force"; Stalin had little response, simply replying that the US should "use it on the Japanese."

For decades following, government officials were certain that Stalin's response was one of an uninformed and confused leader who did not fully understand what Truman had told him; but it wasn't until much later, that we found that Stalin's lack of surprise was rather telling. For years Stalin had known of the existence of our atomic weapon program thanks to the infiltration of Soviet spies within our nuclear programs. And he didn't just *know of it*; the USSR was devising its own atomic weapons program at the time, using blueprints stolen from the US program.

And it wasn't just naïveté on our part; the Soviets were actually one step ahead of us, using methods that just made us look silly. While we were setting up wiretaps to catch them discussing plans on the phone, they were encrypting notes into code inscribed on the wrapper of a stick of chewing gum. If we blew our cover, their evidence was edible and gone before we even had a chance to know what we were looking for.

Because of these techniques, Soviet information traveled slowly and surreptitiously; we were caught off guard because we assumed that things would be moving faster due to the modern technology available at the time. The Soviets moved in the shadows, setting up drops and sharing information almost under our noses.

Nothing about this was easy on Americans. Somehow,

knowing that the USSR was operating using such old methods in secret made things more difficult. Nothing just *happened*, it was drawn out over a long period, done in hiding and leaving questions in its wake. Perhaps worst of all was that we really had no idea who was actually doing this—and neither did our government. This resulted in a paranoia that only served to multiply the fears that were already so pervasive. Not only could everything be taken from you in an instant, but it could be your neighbor or coworker carrying out the orders to do so.

This was worrying in many regards, but also entirely emblematic of the dissonance we were experiencing at the time with the danger of being simultaneously under- and overinformed. We didn't know what we didn't know, but which was worse: knowing that we didn't know, or the not knowing itself? While either option is just as upsetting, Americans were put in a really difficult place; the situation required immense trust in a government that many of us felt we couldn't fully trust. The government had just taken us through World War II, the Korean War, and the Vietnam War, with the result being the death of American soldiers in the tens of thousands.

What could really be done, though? In a secretive nuclear arms race, we were unable to enact change or call both sides to a truce. It didn't really work like that. Short of gathering up your family, selling your home, and beginning your new life as mountain hermits far enough from society to be unaffected by whatever nuclear devastation might be wrought on major cities, you were just stuck.

The longer the Cold War progressed, the more often we found ourselves stuck in this anxiety-inducing middle ground, the more that uneasy feeling built up. Instead of getting easier as time went on, it became more and more difficult, building like a boiling pot of water. We were approaching the upper boundary of what the public could endure, the point of no return.

For every meeting you went to, every family dinner or children's soccer game where everything went as planned, there was an equal moment in an alternate universe where you looked to the sky to imagine missiles streaking down, other missiles leaving just as quickly as we would return fire, knowing all was lost but hoping to send a message just the same. At any moment you could potentially go from a moment spent with family around the TV watching *Dallas* to a crater where your house once was. Mutually assured destruction could occur at a moment's notice, and there was nothing you could do about it.

For Americans, this was life for decades. This was the Cold War.

Atari: The Early Gaming Pioneers

2

WALK WITH ME ON A TRIP DOWN MEMORY LANE, WON'T you? It's 1979, *The Empire Strikes Back* is mere months away, and everyone is losing their damn minds about it. Game arcades are hot, but stagnation in the arcade product has left consumers unsure of its long-term value. As a result, it hasn't yet become the staple of American pop culture it will just a few years later, attracting kids and teens to their favorite machines to play away their quarters in hopes of breaking that ridiculously challenging, there's-no-way-he-actually-did-that high score. There's no *Gauntlet* or *Pac-Man* yet, but you can play *Space Wars* (unappealing), *Death Race* (even more unappealing), or the newest hit, *Breakout*, paving the way for the great arcade classics still to come.

Look, it's not great at this point; but progress is coming fast.

Video games are already grabbing the attention of kids everywhere, and word has gotten around that Atari is finally bringing its top arcade hits to home consoles, making the Atari Video Computer System the hottest ticket of the 1979 holiday season. It had been out for a few years at this point, but now the best of the arcade is finally coming with it—that's more than enough to cause a stir. It is pandemonium for parents and pure joy for kids—*if* you can get your hands on one, that is. Maybe you'll be one of the few lucky enough to wake up or come home to that perfectly wrapped giant box, knowing exactly what it is yet still fearing that you're getting your hopes up and, in fact, you'll end up with another boring old toy. *Boring old toy?* What kid thinks that way? Anyone who has played *Pong* and *Super Breakout*, that's who. That's how powerful Atari is; there's been nothing like it before. Home consoles are but a vision of the future; we don't yet have Sega Genesis, the Nintendo Entertainment System, or affordable home computers, so this is groundbreaking. And everybody wants one.

Now, if it weren't for the Atari Video Computer System, you'd be all over that Starship *Enterprise* model, but not this year—oh no, that might as well be a pet rock for all you're concerned. The Starship *Enterprise* is what the other kids are getting, but you want the Atari Video Computer System. The games aren't anything like they are in the arcades; they're simple and basic, but that doesn't matter. Sure, action figures and toys are fun, but playing *Pong* and *Space Invaders* in the comfort of your own home? That's revolutionary, and it's something not every kid can do.

But we're getting a little ahead of ourselves. Let's go back to how Atari actually got its start.

In 1972, Nolan Bushnell and Ted Dabney founded Syzygy Engineering, where they created the world's first commercially available arcade video game, *Computer Space*. This was based on the 1961 game *Spacewar!* by Steve Russell, which is widely regarded as *the* first digital video game.

As an engineering student at the University of Utah, Bushnell had seen the game running on the university mainframe in the late 1960s and was obsessed. *Spacewar!* tasked two players with piloting opposing ships, facing off in a death match while attempting to fight gravity pulling them into the sun. It was a hit. He instantly knew how something as special as this could change the future, and knew that he needed to do whatever he could to see this marvelous invention reach the masses.

The main issue was price. Very few computers were capable of even running the game, and those that were came at a high cost. The setup that Steve Russell first developed the game on? It was the DEC PDP-1, a $140,000 computer and display bundle—an extremely expensive purchase in 1961, even for a university. He wanted to find some way to get the costs down enough to bring it to the public, but knew that it just wasn't feasible with the current financials. Dismayed as he was that it wasn't something that he could start working on right away, he didn't give up, always keeping an eye out for how he might be able to accomplish this down the road as the technology became more affordable.

A few years later, fresh out of college, Bushnell found his first engineering job at Ampex, a Silicon Valley technology company pioneering audio and video recording technology, where he was paired up with Ted Dabney as an office mate. The two became friends right away, finding each other's intellectual and analytical approach to thinking easy to connect with. They knew about different areas of computing—Bushnell knew programming, while Dabney focused on hardware design—and used this to learn from each other, inquiring with each other to learn about how they might approach a situation.

During this time, Bushnell met another Silicon Valley engineer, Jim Stein, and the two quickly became friends. Stein worked at Stanford University's Artificial Intelligence Lab, and in passing conversation mentioned to Bushnell that the lab had a PDP-6 in its possession. Bushnell was struck with excitement, immediately asking if they could head back to the lab to play *Spacewar!* And that they did—from that point on, a lot.

Back at Ampex, Bushnell and Dabney's relationship began to flourish. Sharing an office, they spent the whole day together and soon began blowing off work to play chess and chat. It was during this time that they began to share their ambitions and ideas with each other—using each other's strengths to explore how they might make things work. As they continued to play together, they get tired of chess, instead taking up the Chinese strategy game Go, the oldest board game still in play today. Though Go was simple to understand, the complexities of the game challenged the two of them and allowed them to really put their minds to use.

One afternoon Bushnell decided he was over chess and Go and decided to take Dabney to see *Spacewar!* at the Stanford lab. While it was all Bushnell could think about, Dabney didn't find it too interesting, but he knew that if someone like Bushnell was interested, there had to be something to it, even if he didn't see it right away. As it turned out, they still couldn't afford the computers required to make it work outside of a computer lab, and the idea died on the vine. That is, until Bushnell made a startling discovery.

What if they didn't need an expensive computer to run the game? As Dabney recounted the realization in an interview with *Technologizer*, "Nolan came to me one time and he said, 'On a TV set, when you turn the vertical hold on the TV, the picture will go up, and if you turn it the other way, it goes down. Why does it do that?' I explained it to him. It was the difference between the sync and the picture timing. He said, 'Could we do that with some control?' I said, 'Yeah, we probably can, but we'd have to do it digitally, because analog would not be linear.'"

And that was the moment where they figure out how to make this work. They didn't need an expensive computer for each instance of the game, but could instead make their own hardware that allowed the user to control the changes in signal using an input. Dabney made quick work of the idea and completed a prototype that allowed the player to interact with a dot on the screen, moving it as the television refreshed. With this technology in hand, the two set off to make Bushnell's vision of a commercially viable *Spacewar!* a reality.

It would take many years for the two to fully work through the issues. They were strapped for capital and eventually needed to sign a deal to help cover manufacturing and development costs. They signed a deal with Nutting Associates, a local coin-op game distributor that agreed to cover these costs in exchange for a royalty and Bushnell's employment (Dabney did join, but later), to produce a single-player version of the game, *Computer Space*. They finished the game in 1971 and released it to high praise—despite only producing a few thousand units.

This may have been small in Nutting's eyes, but for Bushnell it was a sign of the possibilities to come. Knowing that Nutting would struggle to adapt to modern advances without him, Bushnell proposed part ownership of the company for his contributions, Nutting declined, and the two decided to leave, believing they could do better on their own now that they knew what they were doing . . . or at least they thought they did.

And as a result, Atari, Inc. was born on June 27, 1972. Little did they know, within a decade, that Atari would become a technology powerhouse with more than ten thousand employees and an annual revenue of more than $2 billion.

SOON AFTER STARTING Atari (a name taken from a move in the game Go that signaled when a player's pieces were about to be engulfed by the other, and a name that Bushnell found very symbolic of the rest of the industry), the two realized they were going to need more help if they were to be successful at this. They convinced Al Alcorn, one of their former coworkers from

Ampex, to join them to build a prototype for them to sell to a manufacturer, similar to what they had done with *Computer Space*.

Alcorn agreed, thinking they already had contracts in place, as Bushnell led him to believe was the case. They needed something that would do much larger numbers than *Computer Space* and was more easily accessible—it fell on Bushnell to figure out just what this might be. "I had to come up with a game people already knew how to play," said Bushnell in an interview for *Zap!: The Rise and Fall of Atari* in 1984; "something so simple that any drunk in a bar could play."

Just a month before quitting Nutting, Bushnell had seen the announcement of the Magnavox Odyssey, the world's first games console releasing later that year. The Odyssey was a breakthrough machine, using similar analog technology to what Dabney had developed a few years earlier. Lifelong technology inventor Ralph Baer had, unbeknownst to Bushnell and Dabney, been working on the same projects during the same time period they were, but neither was successful enough to really break through into a commercial market. The Odyssey included two paddles and twelve games, allowing players to engage in very simple gameplay, utilizing three controllable dots and varying overlays to create that gameplay. As part of this announcement, Magnavox was giving the public select opportunities to experience the platform prior to its release. One of these opportunities was somewhat nearby.

Bushnell and a few other coworkers at Nutting took a trip to Burlingame, California, to experience the console firsthand. They played the games that were included with the console and were able to watch as others experienced video games for the first time. It was during this trip that Bushnell found the baseline for which Atari needed to strive: the Odyssey's *Table Tennis*. It was a basic game that tasked players, displayed as white dots, to hit the ball, another white dot, back and forth until someone missed—similar to real table tennis. It was extremely basic, but they knew that was what most people were gravitating toward at the time. Part of why *Computer Space* had failed to gain more adoption was the difficulty of play—it was hard to control, and newcomers often had difficulty understanding how to play. Everyone knew how to play table tennis, he surmised; they should just make games that anyone could pick up and play.

Once Alcorn was on board, Bushnell recalled his time with the *Table Tennis* game and asked Alcorn to make him something similar, hiding the fact that this was just a test of his skills and not the project they were hired to create. Alcorn made easy work of this basic request, finding that, with his own improvements to Bushnell's *Computer Space* hardware, the game came together relatively quickly. The digital nature of the project allowed for many improvements over the Odyssey's hardware, feeling more like a programmed engagement than a series of analog signals being sent back and forth. As a result, it felt slow—Alcorn knew they needed to make some improvements to the core gameplay if they didn't want to bore players to death.

They broke the player's cursor into multiple parts, allowing the ball to interact with the paddle in unique ways, bouncing at different angles instead of just directly back and forth. They also added a mechanism that increased the ball's speed over time, forcing there to be an eventual end to the game; as players progressed, the game would continually speed up until one player was unable to keep up. They also added scoring, which players had previously been required to keep on their own.

Bushnell also wanted them to have sound effects—the Magnavox Odyssey didn't. He knew that sound was a vital component to immersing players in the experience; it would also one-up the Odyssey, which he didn't mind either. Alcorn, still new to the process, didn't know how to accomplish this. He knew how to create digital graphics, but sounds were a whole new thing. Thinking back to his time at Ampex, he did some digging and found that a readily available component within their board, a sync generator responsible for ensuring that video signals were sent out properly, could actually generate basic noises on demand. So that's what he went with. Bushnell said he wanted "the roar of a crowd of thousands," explained Alcorn in a 2008 interview with IGN, but he had no idea how to accomplish that. Instead, he just made the simplest sound he could and moved on. "There's the sound—if you don't like it, *you* do it!" he told Bushnell—and that's exactly how it stayed, birthing some of the most iconic sounds in gaming history.

Now that the design was out of the way, it was time for them to put the cabinet together. He purchased a small television, built a four-foot wooden cabinet to house everything, added a laundromat coin slot with a milk jug to collect coins, and soldered the boards in place. It was quick and somewhat crude, but they had accomplished the entire project to this point in just two months. While Bushnell had originally intended for it to be nothing but a test of Alcorn's skills, he found it to be great fun and exactly what he was looking for all those years ago. They spent hours playing the early prototype and settled on the name *Pong*.

Believing that it could be successful if done properly, they reached out to a local bar, Andy Capp's Tavern in Sunnyvale, to see if they could place the *Pong* prototype next to the bar's other games as a test. They had worked with tavern manager Bill Gattis before through their pinball dealings, and Gattis agreed to let them test their prototype. Less than a month later, in September 1972, Alcorn and Bushnell delivered the machine themselves, setting it up on one of the wine barrels the bar used for tables.

As a way to supplement their income, Atari had begun taking orders for pinball machines, knowing they could buy and maintain the machines inexpensively. At the time, they could own a "route" of stores, a similar process to vending machines, that allowed them to place the machines and earn the revenue without having to cover the overhead that the rest of the business required. It was a low-cost effort that became extremely profitable for them, allowing them to fund their video game adventure and create contacts that would be invaluable down the road, such as Bill Gattis.

Alcorn and Bushnell sat at the bar, drinking a beer and waiting for anyone to come up and play. Eventually they got two players who were willing to give their quarter to an unknown machine—this was a big deal considering it was placed alongside a pinball machine and *Computer Space*, two much more familiar staples at Andy Capp's. The two players quickly figured out how to play and found themselves enchanted with the unknown game. Bushnell approached the two, getting their feedback to see what they thought. It was overwhelmingly positive, and Alcorn and Bushnell thought they might have finally found a hit.

But beer after beer, people passed the machine without hesitation. Alcorn and Bushnell waited through a few more drinks before realizing that they must have just gotten lucky—it wasn't a hit after all. Dejected, they went home for the night, rethinking their approach. Little did they know it would slowly become a major hit with the crowd and word would spread like wildfire. A few days later, Alcorn received a phone call from Gattis. "Al, this is the weirdest thing. When I opened the bar this morning, there were two or three people at the door waiting to get in," recounted Alcorn for Steven Kent's *The Ultimate History of Video Games* (2001). "They walked in and played that machine. They didn't buy anything. I've never seen anything like it before." Despite their false start the first night, things were starting to heat up, and this slow burn had them hopeful about the game's future. But they weren't ready for what was to come.

Two weeks later, Gattis called again—*Pong* had stopped working and he needed Alcorn to come fix it. Alcorn was anticipating getting the call eventually—they had used pretty basic hardware for their initial prototype, so as the game's popularity increased, it was bound to have issues. But when he arrived, the paddles didn't seem to be having any issues. They looked fine. He decided to play a game to see if he could diagnose what the issue was. He opened the coin box to grant himself a free game and was greeted by a flood of quarters overflowing the modified milk jug. The game had been so popular that the sheer number of quarters had caused the game to malfunction. Unable to process what was happening, Alcorn grabbed handfuls of the quarters and started shoving them in his pockets. Realizing just how popular the game had become, he gave Gattis his home number, knowing this would likely continue.

They had a hit on their hands, but now they needed to worry about getting more units manufactured and out to other establishments along their route. They tried to strike a deal with Bally's Midway Manufacturing, with whom they had an existing pinball deal, but Bally was unconvinced of both the game and their success. At that time, a typical coin-op game would bring in roughly fifty dollars a week; *Pong* was doing four times that, even at this early stage. Still, Bally declined to purchase *Pong*.

Once that deal failed to go through, Bushnell knew they had to do it on their own. They took all of the capital they had available to them from *Pong* and their pinball business, about thirty-three hundred dollars, and manufactured an initial run of eleven new machines. This was a huge risk; they knew that *Pong* had been a success in one location, but would others get on board when they had to pay for the nine-hundred-dollar cabinet? As it turned out, the answer was very much yes. Upon completion of the cabinets, they sold all eleven right away, funding a rolling run of fifty more units. Though they were seeing great success, they were still short on funds, space, and manpower.

Upon completion of the fifty orders, Bushnell was able to convince Wells Fargo to give the company a fifty-thousand-dollar loan, thanks to 150 pending orders of *Pong* cabinets, and used part of it to acquire a lease on an abandoned roller-skating rink down the road from their current office that would allow them to expand production capabilities. Now that funds and space were settled, they needed to figure out their people solution. They knew that Alcorn could handle all of the boards and higher-end components, but they still needed people to build the cabinets and assemble everything. There were only three of them; they couldn't do it on their own. They had to start hiring—and fast.

But with only fifty thousand dollars in capital, they couldn't afford to pay craftsmen to put them together; instead they drove to the local unemployment office and told them they'd hire anyone for $1.75 per hour, just over minimum wage, to assemble the cabinets. Under Alcorn's supervision, they hired each and every person the unemployment office would send them—no matter who they were or what skills they had. They had *Pong* cabinets being assembled by members of the Hell's Angels and even heroin addicts; they had such high demand that they couldn't afford to be picky when it came to their workers.

As a result, however, the factory culture at Atari suffered. It became a den of drugs and illegal activity, with almost every employee smoking marijuana while they worked and some even doing heroin during particularly stressful weeks. With long hours necessary to get these cabinets ready for public consumption, workers ran the show, knowing it wouldn't go on without them.

When Atari first started, there was no assembly line. Instead, each worker installed a component, piece-by-piece, until the cabinet was finished. This was an extremely inefficient process that only allowed them to finish ten machines a day. That might sound like a lot, but they received orders for 2,500 *Pong* cabinets in 1973, so getting through ten a day wasn't going to work.

Alcorn, Bushnell, and Dabney eventually figured out how to pull together a more efficient process as the business grew, and they were able to keep up with demand, but as they grew, culture changed in ways they hadn't expected. While they had started small, they were growing larger than ever. They weren't losing what made them special, and they certainly weren't growing any more corporate, but their predicaments were. Decisions that once affected only a small handful of people now affected many. They weren't producing orders of eleven or fifty units anymore, they were producing them in the thousands, with cash payments up front. The game had broken out of the bar scene, finding itself in popular locations like airports and office buildings that wanted to seem high-end. They didn't have the luxury of small-time thinking anymore.

While some were able to adapt, others weren't, and after a tumultuous falling out with Bushnell, Dabney was bought out of the company and retained the company's coin route business. By the end of 1974 they had manufactured more than eight thousand *Pong* machines and were operating at a scale never before imagined by Bushnell.

Yet, even then, they continued to operate less like a traditional company and more like a pioneering cooperative. While most board meetings occur in boardrooms, Atari's were conducted in the hot tub of Bushnell's Los Gatos estate. Group planning sessions with white boards and markers were exchanged for bongs and beers as the group sat around sharing ideas. In fact, these planning sessions in the aptly named Grass Valley, California, became such a large part of Atari culture that Bushnell ended up purchasing Cyan Engineering, the tech company where they would often hold corporate retreats for planning sessions, to ensure they maintained a close relationship and could always use the facilities. During these retreats, the board members would get high and try to hash out (pun intended) solutions to the problems that were plaguing their business, whether it was a technical feat or an issue with a competitor.

It was these types of occurrences that set the basis for the culture of Atari and, as far as Bushnell was concerned, was directly responsible for the success they encountered. What they were doing was so different and unique at the time that this level of freedom was required for them to create in a way that made them different from everyone else. By the end of 1974, this uniqueness would be the factor that allowed them to thrive in a market dominated by copycats.

When creating *Pong*, the Atari founders had been so focused on being able to manufacture it that they hadn't managed to secure patents for the technology they had developed. Meanwhile, their competitors were researching the machines to find out everything they could to implement their own clone. By the time *Pong* was successful, there were too many other similar games on the market for a patent to be granted, and they began to realize that Atari's standing in arcades would not live forever. Something new was necessary if they were to survive.

That same year, Alcorn reached out to a former board designer, Harold Lee, who had recently left Atari to inquire about the possibilities of putting *Pong* on a single chip. Lee had been a chip designer prior to working at Atari, and Alcorn felt that he would be the best person to help accomplish the job. The two of them began work on a home version of *Pong* and soon found a way to replicate the same hardware Alcorn had created for the arcade release in a much smaller package that could be placed on a single chip.

The main hurdle became actually selling this home console, as most stores didn't believe it would actually sell—a fair assumption, considering that most home consoles sales at the time were very small. They were able to convince Sears to take a chance on them, though, and they ended up selling 150,000 units for the 1975 holiday season.

This was much larger than anything they had ever manufactured before (and more than double what they had initially proposed), but they were confident they could make it happen, and they did. While they were unsure if there was a large enough market at the time, they were soon validated as the product became the hottest item that holiday season, selling out completely and becoming Sears's highest-selling item ever. Meanwhile, Atari's Coin-Op Division had been producing dozens of other arcade games, though most were different variations of *Pong* that failed to innovate in unique ways and had most of the industry stuck in a state where they assumed that only simple games could be made, that there was no future. Despite Atari's manifesto to always innovate and move forward rather than look backward, the company experienced its own share of failures in this regard, often creating games that didn't sell due to little variation from their predecessors: *Pong* vs. *Super Pong*.

Atari launched thirteen different games in 1974, some through a competitor that Bushnell secretly funded and staffed to get around distributor exclusivity. For as annoyed as he was that competitors were stealing Atari's product ideas, he was fine with using such practices himself if they allowed Atari to increase profits. This was his solution to the copycat problem, to use the increased resources that Atari had over their competitors to outproduce them. If they were going to copy Atari's games, Atari would release a new one every month, something their competitors couldn't even dream of, and this allowed the company to stay one step ahead of the competition.

Bushnell knew Atari could no longer rely on the sales of one style of game; it had to innovate. With the sales of *Home Pong* in hand, it became clear to him that the home console market was the future of gaming, but that the technology wasn't yet there to make it commercially viable at scale, a barrier he once again found himself encountering just as he had with *Pong* a few years earlier.

Atari couldn't keep releasing one-game systems if it was to cement its position in the home console market and begin creating the progress that its founders wanted to see in the whole. The company needed to develop a home console capable of playing multiple games. Once it did this, it would be able to sell people multiple games a year, keep down manufacturing costs, and, since Atari was the most dominant name brand at the time, capture the one coveted spot that most households would have, by the TV, cutting out the competition in the process.

At the same time, the company would continue to flesh out its arcade offerings; this would allow it to build a massive catalog of games that could easily be ported into the home console once it was clear which ones were successful. It was a long-term play, but one that Bushnell believed to be the future for Atari. He didn't want to see arcades die out, but knew that, at least for Atari, the competition was becoming more of a problem with each passing day.

In May 1974 a young Steve Jobs arrived at the doorstop of Atari headquarters asking for a job. Alcorn wasn't sure whether to hire him or call the cops, but eventually he gave Jobs a chance. He didn't have any real experience, and Alcorn wasn't even sure if Jobs had the skills to do anything for them, but he saw Jobs's passion and decided it was worth a shot. He quickly found himself questioning if it was worth it, however, as Jobs began annoying the other employees of Atari whom he deemed to be "incompetent." Alcorn's solution was to have Jobs work at Atari during the night shift, when the other engineers weren't around.

Bushnell and Steve Bristow had just finished designing a single-player version of *Pong* and needed someone to create the prototype. Bushnell was upset with the high production costs mounting over the number of chips used on each board, so he offered a bounty to the person who could design it with the fewest chips. Jobs accepted, despite not knowing how to actually accomplish this.

During his time on the night shift, Jobs would often invite his good friend Steve Wozniak to join him. Once he had accepted the project of designing this single-player game of *Pong* they had named *Breakout*, he enlisted the help of Wozniak to design the board, offering to split the pay with him. Over the course of four sleepless nights, they finished and presented Alcorn with a forty-four-chip version of *Breakout*. It was extremely impressive, and they were awarded the bounty of seven hundred dollars. Little did Wozniak know, however, that Jobs had been given an additional five thousand dollars for the job, which he didn't share between the two.

While still working at Atari and Hewlett-Packard, Jobs and Wozniak began creating their own version of the home computer. Believing it to be the future of modern technology, they soon left their respective jobs and started their own company, Apple.

Atari was offered the Apple II prior to Jobs and Wozniak doing it on their own, but Atari wasn't interested. They were in the business of making video game hardware, and the personal computer market was too niche for it to be a profitable business, at least at the time. However, they would be happy to supply Apple with all the components needed for the Apple II, as Jobs and Wozniak couldn't get their own trade accounts.

Alcorn was happy to do it, selling to them for 15% above cost. He liked them, even if he considered them "fun little guys, but harmless." In fact, they thought the chances of Apple succeeding were so small that both Alcorn and Bushnell declined to invest in the formation of Apple at 33% for $50,000, with Alcorn telling Jobs, "I got enough wallpaper, but I'll take a free computer." He did go on to get that computer, and still has it to this day, but would much rather have the wallpaper.

Following the success of *Home Pong* in 1975, Bushnell immediately commissioned the engineers from Cyan Engineering to begin work on creating the Atari Video Computer System, or VCS (later renamed the Atari 2600), to handle this monumental task. They quickly began prototyping out other options and realized just how feasible this could be. If they were able to build a unit that didn't rely on custom logic boards (as did most arcade units) but instead housed only its own central processing unit, display, memory, and sound board, allowing the games to be stored on removable memory units, this could all work just fine.

Up to this point, most removable games platforms had used paper tape to store the game programs on them, but that wouldn't work for the games that Atari was now creating. The company wanted to be able to use memory of some kind—with the popular options being cassette tapes and floppy disks. But Atari engineers found that they could simulate a cartridge-based system simply by housing the storage with a connector inside a thick plastic housing; this would give the appearance of an expensive product while being inexpensive to manufacture. It was also more durable and consumer-friendly, so they knew that it would increase its value even more.

As a result, they would be able to sell these games, which cost ten dollars to design and manufacture, for thirty dollars each. This allowed Atari to offset the low profitability of the system and form the basis for the gaming industry, which today follows a very similar model.

Despite these cost-saving measures, sales of *Pong* had dipped so low that Atari wouldn't be able to cover production costs for the unit. The company needed to find some way to raise the capital required to make it happen; this was the last hope for recovering and steering the company toward the future Bushnell so wholeheartedly believed in. Rather than attempting to acquire traditional funding, Bushnell proposed two options: go public or sell the company to someone who shared its vision.

Unfortunately, the timing just didn't work out. The United States had just exited a recession prompted by President Richard Nixon's policy decisions and was in a fragile economic state. In an attempt to cut down on unemployment, Nixon had pressured the Federal Reserve to disallow the conversion of gold into US dollars, prompting an eventual 40 percent decline in the US stock market. Things were starting to recover, but there was still too much uncertainty for the Atari board members to feel comfortable with. As a result, they chose instead to find a private company that would be interested in buying them. With that they'd be able to get the capital they needed to produce the VCS without having to worry about outside pressures.

The decline in interest in video games following the endless clones of *Pong* had major companies wondering if home console gaming was just another fad that wouldn't last, an assessment Bushnell didn't entirely disagree with. At the same time that he was trying to secure funding for the VCS, he had also created a pinball division at Atari specifically focused on creating new machines for the again burgeoning pinball market. He hoped this division would serve to hedge any big bets that they were looking to make on home console gaming in case, yet again, the public wasn't ready for that.

They were cautious to invest, but found a suitable partner in Warner Communications, a staple of the growing entertainment industry that was looking to expand its offerings to video games. Warner was on board with the vision that Bushnell proposed and offered $28 million for the company. It was a no-brainer, and in October 1976 Atari was sold to Warner, with Bushnell remaining at the helm of the company. Warner believed in what he had done and the vision he had for the future; there was no reason to replace him.

With newly secured funds and a renewed vision for the future, Bushnell and crew pushed forward, releasing the VCS in October 1977, just a year after the acquisition. It was a whole new era for them. They had what felt like unlimited resources, and regularly took trips on the company Gulf Stream. "Life was good," as Alcorn put it. They suddenly had the money to do the things they wanted to do, both personally and in the business. They could both create the VCS and purchase a 1965 AC Cobra muscle car (which Alcorn did almost immediately following the acquisition).

Unfortunately, a lot had happened in the span of that year; multiple competitors had released products into a market already suffering from oversaturation. With too many options and too few buyers, none of these home consoles found success, and the market began to decline even further than it already had.

After a disappointing first year, Warner was concerned. The VCS has seen slow sales and there wasn't any sign of them increasing to the point that was expected. Sales weren't terrible, but this certainly wasn't the dream Warner had been sold when it acquired Atari. Warner thought every household in America would be lining up to get a VCS, but instead found it unable to penetrate the mainstream culture barrier. The company began to reevaluate its options, wondering if it should just cut its losses and abandon Atari.

Warner wasn't the only one who felt this way. Bushnell was disappointed with the failure of the VCS and pushed for Atari to move on to new products. He wasn't exactly sure what those might be at the time, but he knew there had to be something out there that could give Atari the advantage over the thick competition.

In order to help solve this predicament, Warner hired Ray Kassar, a former textile executive, to help understand what the company should be doing with Atari. Should Warner get rid of it entirely, or should it figure out how to right the ship and double down? That was for Kassar to find out, but it wouldn't be a walk in the park.

From the very start, it was clear that Bushnell and Kassar weren't going to get along. They were two very different people, on opposite ends of every spectrum imaginable. Bushnell wore T-shirts, often drinking and smoking marijuana in the office, while Kassar wore tailored suits and didn't come to work to get high. These clashes occurred early on, causing much tension.

Yet despite all this Kassar was hopeful. He had tried the VCS and believed it to be the future.

Meanwhile, Bushnell wanted to look to the future, doubling down on the pinball division by creating unique game tables that others couldn't afford to make and selling off all remaining stock of the VCS immediately so they could focus on future iterations of their home console product. He felt that the crowded market and poor performance were indicators enough that they should be focusing their attentions elsewhere. "We wanted to build the next generation," said Alcorn of the meeting, "That was the way we did it. We obsoleted our product." They didn't want to rely on the VCS to carry them forever. "We'll make a bigger, faster, better one." But Warner disagreed, and Kassar recommended focusing on building out the VCS lineup, which he felt would sell exceptionally well that holiday season rather than abandoning the console at the height of its success. Bushnell disagreed, telling Kassar and the rest of the board that they were "a bunch of idiots," recalls Alcorn. They didn't like that very much and knew they were going to have a problem on their hands.

After this meeting, Bushnell attempted to circumvent the Warner board members and make the decision on his own. Warner found out and immediately relieved Bushnell of his duties as CEO, replacing him with Kassar, who they believed could help steer Atari toward a more profitable future.

Bushnell was oddly calm about this ousting. He had other projects he wanted to work on and knew that he couldn't go on in a company that didn't follow the ideals that he had created. "I got increasingly uncomfortable with management style of Warner," he told me, explaining what caused the rift between the two halves. "I think those guys were not used to being called dumb shits," he said, laughing, "And I kinda did that a little bit too much." It wasn't even really about this argument. He knew that they wanted him gone and that they would find another way to do it, so he went quietly.

As a result of his removal as CEO, Bushnell's noncompete clause forced him to leave gaming for the next seven years, giving him the opportunity to work on another passion project he had been trying to figure out for the last decade. He had always been perplexed by the stigma attached to video games, that they couldn't possibly be fun for anyone other than drunks and dropouts; he knew it was more about the environment the games were often found in than the games themselves, and wanted to find a solution to fix this. Unable to create gaming consoles, he set off building out the plan for what would eventually become the family entertainment restaurant Chuck E. Cheese's.

He wanted to create an environment where kids could get together with their friends and experience new arcade games together. Video games were all about discovery and imagination, something that aligned very well with how kids typically approach things, so he knew it would be the perfect fit. As it turns out, Chuck E. Cheese's became one of the premier birthday and celebration destinations for children and teenagers for the better part of three decades, helping to solidify arcade gaming as an experiential hobby even as home console gaming became more prevalent.

Bushnell turned out to be right for the 1978 holiday season, with less than 70 percent of Atari's 550,000 VCS units selling through retailers. This was a devastating blow to Atari and Kassar, who had believed things would finally be turning in their favor. Instead they were treated to their second consecutive failed year in a row, increasing tensions around an already concerning investment for Warner. Bushnell, wanting to prove his theory, shorted Warner Communications stock and saw great success as he earned more from that short position than from the sale of Atari to Warner. Despite reservations, they held strong and remained focused on Kassar's vision for the future.

As vindicated as Bushnell must have felt, he couldn't predict that the revival of the VCS was just around the bend. In 1979 Atari released *Adventure*, a multiscreen adventure game that opened the eyes of many to the degrees to which gaming could go. Players were no longer relegated to *Pong* clones and simple sports games, but could instead experience a whole new world in the comfort of their own homes.

For many, it was the first time that video games felt real, like they could go on to become more than just a momentary escape from reality and develop into something much larger. This not only surprised consumers but also other developers at Atari; they became heavily influenced by *Adventure* and began thinking much bigger when creating games. They were no longer just re-creating things that were already popular in the gaming world; they were now creating entirely new worlds and pushing the hardware beyond previous limits.

By the end of 1979, the VCS had gone on to sell a million units, nearly doubling the previous year's sales and becoming the best-selling item that year. Though it was just the start of the VCS's dominance, Kassar knew they made the right choice, and he proceeded to double down on Atari's efforts toward building great games for both the VCS and arcades.

Yet despite this success, the rest of the folks at Atari weren't convinced that Kassar was the best leader for them, signaling a massive change in how the Consumer Division felt from the inside. It wasn't the same Atari they had helped build under Bushnell's direction. Key members of the organization, including almost every early Atari member who had worked to create the fledgling arcade business, began to depart the company, citing difficulties adapting to Kassar's ever-evolving shift in culture away from the Atari they had once loved. This shake-up—upsetting and something that Kassar wishes, in retrospect, he had worked to deter—would leave many of Atari's younger programmers' confidence in the company shaken despite its continued meteoric rise.

"He fucked everything up," Bushnell bluntly puts it. In the eyes of everyone who had been there since the early days, this strong shift in culture led astray the driving force that had made Atari the powerhouse it had once been. They were losing steam, most just couldn't see it yet.

It was a scary time, one they weren't entirely sure how to feel about. They had come to Atari hoping to be a part of the famous culture that thrived on creativity and innovation, but as more of that began to dissolve, they wondered what the future might hold. It was still Atari, and those who remained were more than happy to be there making games that reached more players than ever before, but those who had worked with the company's visionary leaders began to worry about the company's increasing focus on profitability as a cornerstone of the Warner Communications business.

They knew a business needed to make money, and definitely didn't want to trade the freedom they were afforded by Atari's financial success for the old atmosphere, but just questioned whether Kassar was the one best equipped to lead them. He wore three-piece suits and came to work in a limousine: that didn't sound like Atari to them. Atari was about getting high with your friends and creating games the world had never thought possible, all the while having as much fun as possible. It just didn't seem like a good fit, and left them wondering how the company might continue to change under Kassar's leadership. Would the Atari they had come to know and love be gone forever in favor of one that was more profitable? Potentially. But Kassar was undeterred, and continued to focus on the VCS, which he believed to be the future of the company.

Ironically, in ignoring the coin-op side of the business, Kassar essentially allowed it to operate independently. While the Coin-Op Division didn't get any of the praise for the success of its work, it was also allowed to just do its own thing. Kassar didn't want anything to do with it, so it was given free rein to build its own culture, one that flew in stark contrast to the consumer side of the business and allowed Coin-Op to thrive.

Through this many were able to hold on to Bushnell's sense of creativity and innovation, doing all they could to stay faithful to the core tenets of what made Atari great, despite Kassar's influence; it was a move that ultimately resulted in the creation of some of the best arcade games ever made.

Coin-Op's Revenge

3

A S ODD AS IT MAY SOUND LOOKING BACK, ATARI'S COIN-OP Division, led by Lyle Rains, began to feel like a bit of an outcast from the very company it helped create. The Coin-Op developers were the ones who would come up with unique ideas, figure out how to get them implemented, tune the gameplay until it was just right, and get fans to fall in love with the game, but Kassar would give all the credit to the Consumer Division when the bare-bones ports (which were often inferior, due to hardware limitations) succeeded on the Atari Video Computer System, or VCS. It was extremely frustrating for them at the time, and left them feeling like second-class citizens when they were actually responsible for the majority of the creative work that went into each project.

Because of this, they felt like they had the right to push back a little bit. If Kassar wasn't going to give them the attention they deserved, they were going to take it . . . one way or another. Unfortunately for Kassar, the ways in which they decided to go about this weren't always the epitome of productivity.

Just as the early days of Atari had felt a lot like the Wild West, these new days in the Coin-Op Division gave off a similar vibe. When you were first hired as a programmer at Atari, you were given an office, a development console, and a big pile of development tutorials written by other programmers at the company and were told to make an idea happen in the next six months. That was it. No one really came to check on you once you started on a project, and they certainly didn't regularly give advice as to where you should start. You just did your own thing and, if all went well, delivered a finished product in six months.

It wasn't meant to be unorganized or disheveled in this regard, but rather to emphasize the sense of freedom and self-ownership in your product that working in the Coin-Op Division provided. This method was more of a motivator than anything else, but it often caught new programmers off guard, as they felt they had to perform, big time, to see their first game through to completion. The Coin-Op Division wanted you to feel like this project was all yours and that its success and failures were ultimately your responsibility.

That's easier said than done, of course, but with Gene Lipkin at the helm, it felt like Coin-Op really believed it. Whatever you wanted to do, as long as it was sound and you believed it would succeed, you were encouraged to do. It was your project, and it was up to you to make it happen. Sure, you weren't always the singular programmer as the projects began to grow in size, but many still found themselves to be the sole arbiter of their destiny within the industry, and that excited them.

They'd immediately get to work on an existing idea they had, flipping through the book of preapproved ideas, or lighting up a joint to do some thinking. They'd come a long way since the heroin-plagued bathrooms of *Pong*'s production plant, but that didn't mean they were cutting back on the marijuana use— not in the slightest. It was something that Bushnell had always insisted was vital to both the creative process and the culture of Atari at the time—and the Coin-Op developers weren't going to let his legacy go to waste.

Once they had the idea figured out, that's when the hard work began. In these days, you had the tutorials that you were given, but there was still a lot of uncharted territory when it came to programming for a game. When Bushnell departed in 1978, *Adventure* hadn't even been released and many of the company's most impactful advances were still to come, demonstrating just how much there was left to learn. When you didn't know how to do something, you just had to keep trying until it worked, no matter how close to madness it drove you.

With tight deadlines and a high pressure to perform, programmers often found working at Atari to be all-consuming. It wasn't a job where you were able to clock in a solid eight hours from nine to five and then enjoy a nice weekend with your family. If you were working on a project at Atari, that project became your life. Long hours and endless trial and error made for an environment that thrived on camaraderie: you were all in it together, all encountering the same issues and working the same long hours trying to create the same excitement for a player, even if you were all working on different projects.

It may sound like a terrible environment, but that couldn't be farther from how those working there actually felt. Sure, it had its negatives, but they were creating the future of entertainment and were having fun doing it; they wouldn't have traded that for anything in the world. This was, after all, Atari; what could be better?

At the height of development on a project, it wasn't uncommon to find people staying at the office for days at a time, only stopping work to get a few hours of sleep curled up under their desks in the early morning. They'd wake up, roll up a joint on the way to lunch, and get back at it. That was the culture at the time. It's unlike anything seen today in working America, but it worked for Atari—and would soon become the basis for Silicon Valley culture in the late 1970s and early 1980s.

Though the revelry was much more modest than in the company's beginnings, it was the continuation of the party-filled nights and days that Bushnell had implemented years earlier even as the company transitioned to a more corporate setting with its acquisition by Warner Communications.

The more Atari grew, the more traditional entertainment and manufacturing executives were brought in, changing the company's culture one piece at a time. But for now, the Coin-Op programmers were happy to keep doing as they had always done. It was an environment you couldn't find anywhere else, and this had always been one of Bushnell's greatest hopes: to create something so unique that people were willing to sacrifice to be a part of it. It was a testament to how badly these programmers wanted to be a part of the culture. The company was at the forefront of the future and of innovation, at least under Bushnell's direction, and that meant something to people, especially during such a revolutionary period.

Deadlines were fair: you often had multiple months to complete a project, but often the culture itself became a blocker to productivity. The relaxed nature of their working environment often led to days where programmers would spend more time getting high and pulling pranks around the office than actually working. No one really cared that they were doing this, but for as much as they enjoyed having fun, they took their work even more seriously. You could have all the fun you wanted, but your game was going to be done when you said it was—otherwise there would be consequences. With such easy distractions as prevalent as they were, all-nighters quickly became commonplace so that programmers could meet deadlines and actually ship games.

Yet despite the sleepless nights and cold comfort of an early morning nap on the office floor, no one complained. They loved what they were doing. These people weren't asked to trade their lives for their work; they lined up to do so, something that Bush-nell always referred to as "a sign that they were doing something right." Continuing long after his departure from the company, this process would become symptomatic of what Atari would continue to represent throughout the golden age of arcade gaming. Atari was *the* spot to work at if you wanted to make games that people would play, and the company eventually controlled more than seventy-five percent of the gaming market. If you wanted to make games, the sacrifice was worth it.

This wasn't one programmer's bad work habits becoming revisionist history, either. It was, in fact, pervasive throughout the culture that emphasized Bushnell's "work hard, play hard" mentality. Sure, you might spend some sleepless nights at the office, but you were creating the future—so you had a few beers, slept it off, and kept on working.

It was a fun, outrageous, completely unprofessional workplace that resulted in some of the most revolutionary and popular video games the world has ever seen. Behind those massive successes were programmers, and at Atari, those programmers ruled the world; this mentality often carried over into other aspects of office life. If they wanted to get a game of foam football going across their cubicles, they would. They had free run of the place and did as they pleased; no one was going to tell them to stop. It didn't matter if Steven Spielberg himself was walking through the office, they would continue doing whatever they wanted to do.

This was, quite obviously, a massive frustration for Kassar, who was attempting to repair Atari's reputation and gain support from other aspects of the entertainment industry, all of whom were much more buttoned up than even the Coin-Op Division's best. Even with Atari's notoriety and penchant for success, there still needed to be businesspeople who could ensure everything else was running smoothly, so that once the games were finally done, they could get them out the door.

Both Kassar and his upper-management staff would take industry executives on tour of the campus, and visitors always wanted to see the famous Coin-Op Division. When they did, they were greeted with programmers goofing off and causing a ruckus while upper management tried to show these outside executives what they were working on. In reality, it looked like the answer was somewhere along the lines of "not a whole lot," but the Coin-Op developers kept putting out games, and much faster than anyone else in the market.

From the outside looking in, most assumed that a company as dominant as Atari had to be run like a tight ship from top to bottom, but in reality that couldn't have been farther from the truth. It's true, some areas were more focused on moving the business toward a professional attitude than others, but that didn't stop the holdovers from Bushnell's days from carrying on the legacy that he had built in the company. He had created something that didn't run like a traditional business and encouraged individual contribution, while still retaining the benefits that a professional organization could provide. This brought the backbone Atari would need as a company to succeed overall, with strong focus on extremely professional production and manufacturing, but it let the Coin-Op Division run on its own, pushing through without the structure its developers had so purposefully avoided for so long. As much disdain as Kassar had for the way the unit functioned, he knew better than to meddle too hard with success. After all, Coin-Op was forming the basis for the successful VCS home console projects, even if he didn't want to admit it at the time.

Because of this, Coin-Op was able to get away with pretty much anything. It was an office filled with pranks, constant interruptions of people yelling about one thing or another, and, of course, "smoke breaks." At the end of the day, though, work still came first. It just meant that the end of the day wasn't the same time as it was for software engineers down the road. It was much, much later.

Each developer had his or her individual deadlines, and met them no matter what the cost—and there was a cost, but that cost just didn't seem to matter as much to those at Atari. They enjoyed being there. For so many of them, they felt at home. They were able to show off their crazy personalities and be the truest version of themselves without having to worry about management thinking they were just a little too over the top. Because they didn't have to worry about any of this, they were able to express themselves in a much more natural way, unafraid of conflicting with corporate culture or those around them who disagreed. They were able to focus solely on their mission to create, free from the judgment of those around them. This mission was empowering: they felt as if they could try anything in the world and didn't have to worry about whether it made sense or not. As long as the game ended up in the best state for the player, people really weren't concerned how it got there. This created a sense of family in which many felt they had found where they finally belonged, and this had been Bushnell's exact vision from the start.

Since the very beginning, this had always been a major priority for Bushnell: if they were going to spend almost all their time together, they might as well become friends in the process. One way that he attempted to reward employees and kick this off was the weekly party. Every Friday afternoon, without fail, Bushnell would throw a huge party that brought everyone together to celebrate the completion of another week. They were working really long hours, and he knew how challenging that could be on people, so he wanted to make sure they knew how much he appreciated them. They'd grab a lot of beer and take a break from whatever they were working on. It was a time to grow relationships and really get to know the people you saw twenty hours a day.

There was another motivator for this too, though: deloading. Bushnell knew the work was difficult, but he didn't want people to become overwhelmed by it. If you didn't find some time to unwind, it was really easy to break down, which would set the project back as you recovered. He wanted to implement some forced downtime as a part of his "work hard, play hard" motto. If you gave people time to play, they were essentially required to take a break, allowing them to clear their heads and go back to it in a few hours with a fresh mind-set, ready to keep working. Deloading is a form of preparation employed by weight lifters in which they force themselves to take downtime—not to regress, but to prepare themselves for even harder work yet to come for which they would need to be able to operate at a higher level than ever before.

Bushnell wanted you to be able to have a drink and converse with your coworkers, but the real purpose behind it all was to give you these moments of relaxation to increase the amount of work you were then able to complete. As a result, people were willing to work harder and longer at Atari than almost anywhere else, because they knew there was always something crazy, silly, and fun right around the corner.

Yet despite all this fun, the work was very serious. They had cultivated an environment based on fun and family, but if you couldn't do your job, you couldn't work at Atari. It was one of the hottest companies in the world; there were hundreds of programmers lined up who would kill to take the job of someone who couldn't perform—and Atari knew it. As far as the company was concerned, there wasn't any room for dead weight, and the leadership at Atari became very skilled at cutting out those who couldn't keep up or find a way to mesh with the culture—despite there being an internal culture clash that would later shake up the core foundation of what Atari had come to be known for.

Everyone wanted to be a part of Atari. You could have fun in a way that no other office did, work with extremely talented, like-minded people, and get paid well to do it. It was the dream, and there was nowhere else that people wanted to be—if you worked at Atari, you did everything you could to stay there.

This is even truer in the context of the time. The United States had just been through multiple recessions and the Cold War was beginning to escalate, with nuclear weapons reaching their peak within the USSR. It was a scary time for the average American. You didn't know if you were safe from nuclear war, let alone whether you would have a job by the end of the year. It wasn't a time for extravagant vacations or purchases. It wasn't a fun time, to say the least, but Atari provided a somewhat safe haven.

Atari provided financial stability, for sure, but there was an emotional stability that came with that. Employees worked in a place built around happiness and creativity, something that many valued more than money at the time—and this was evident in the way they worked. Programmers weren't paid overtime, but that didn't stop them from filling the building (and parking lot) on Saturdays and Sundays. This eventually became an issue, as Atari had to begin paying others to come in on the weekends to keep up with the volume of work the programmers were putting out. After all, it didn't really matter how quickly programmers could work if the engineers weren't there to get the game ready to ship.

As this culture of long hours and full devotion to one's work continued to grow, five twelve-to-sixteen-hour days began to expand spread to seven. Despite Kassar's desire for the opposite, this wasn't a culture based around office hours and strict rules; it was about doing everything you needed to create the best product for the consumer, no matter the cost. The full parking lot on the weekends was less an indicator of how many people came in during the day on the weekends and more about how *few* people were there during normal business hours in the traditional workweek. As working hours stretched longer and longer, many found themselves forgoing sleep in favor of continuing to work, pushing themselves through multiple days of continuous labor without sleep. This often resulted in a cavalcade of different working shifts, with some programmers working for four days straight, then taking a full forty-eight hours to recover before coming back in and doing it all over again.

This full house on the weekends quickly became common, and it speaks volumes of the impact that Atari had on these programmers' lives. It wasn't just about creating great games: it was about giving them somewhere to go where they felt safe. Some people didn't need this and saw it only as a job. For others, it was their shelter from the outside world. After all, if you dedicate yourself entirely to your work, you don't exactly have time to watch the evening news.

When they weren't sleeping, they were in the office working. Any semblance of a work-life balance dissolved for most programmers working at Atari at the time—but that was exactly how both they and Atari wanted it. They were able to escape the terrors of reality, and Atari was able to get more from them than anyone else; it was one of the most productive times in game development history.

These games were, obviously, much smaller in scale than the games we see today, and they often featured only a single programmer, but the concept was simple: give someone the keys to the kingdom, let him run with his idea in a culture based around creativity and hard work, and watch the results flourish. This was an extremely fruitful endeavor for both parties, but proved to be unsustainable in the long term. Many programmers found themselves unable to handle the pressures that came with maintaining such a lifestyle. There were multiple reports of breakdowns from exhaustion during those days, and it's not hard to imagine why. Just as Dave Theurer would soon experience with *Missile Command*, devoting yourself fully to something at this extreme a level often led to intense cases where you could become overwhelmed by your work and find yourself unable to move forward.

But if you were able to get through this, you were rewarded with one of the most creative environments to ever exist, working with some of the smartest creators to grace the gaming industry. Given the opportunity to work with such intelligent people, many often found those first few years at Atari to be some of the most significant in their career from an educational standpoint. Not only were you given the freedom to experiment and test out new things, regardless of whether they made it into the final game, but you were able to work through challenging ideas with those much smarter than you. It bred a culture that relied on creativity and hard work to get the best possible product out of you.

This was key to Atari's success, resulting in some of the most innovative and well-received games to ever be created. The company was able to take people who had never created a game before, give them the tools and peers needed to succeed, and transform them into rock stars capable of creating masterpieces in a matter of months. It was truly extraordinary and unlike anything seen since. Unfortunately, it was also key to Atari's demise.

As The Coin-Op Division's best and brightest continued to grow, they began to realize how vital they were to the success of the company despite their relatively low pay and recognition compared to those in the Consumer Division. It was a difficult place for the company to be in; it had just lost a lot of the major players from the Bushnell days upon his departure, which freed up room for new people to come in, but that also left a lot of ambiguity in how the company was sharing its success with the employees directly responsible for it.

Atari realized it was in a tough place and needed to do something about it. It was earning hundreds of millions of dollars a year, while programmers were often earning around twenty-five thousand dollars, regardless of how successful any game was. There wasn't a bonus program that rewarded them based on the sales of their games, and there certainly weren't major career advancement opportunities coming out of Coin-Op. If Kassar needed new workers, he brought them in from the outside. This limited the options that people felt they had available, which only made things worse.

If your game was a massive success, you were definitely afforded perks that others weren't, giving you the opportunity to choose preferential ideas and projects, but this didn't feel too different from the free-flowing nature of individuality and ownership that already existed within Atari. You still had to make a game that didn't have a direct affect on your compensation, so some felt that Atari was taking advantage of the culture it had created to avoid rewarding those who brought the most value.

This affected not only Coin-Op but also the Consumer Division. Around this time, the VCS was beginning to boom, and sales were exceeding Atari's wildest expectations. The entire company was ecstatic, and Kassar had his team push programmers in both Coin-Op and Consumer to pump out even more titles to continue the company's meteoric rise. Unfortunately, one of the ways Atari did this actually ended up working against it in a pretty major way. To help spark creativity and increase ownership over its projects, Atari's marketing lead sent out an internal memo that detailed sales for the year, game by game, listing each as a percentage of sales. In the mind of the marketing lead, this was an easy way for people to see the most popular titles and use this as inspiration for what might land best with consumers. But doing so inadvertently allowed programmers to see how much (or how little) their one-person game had earned, pushing some to recognize their direct contribution to Atari was worth more than a hundred times their current salary. For many of these programmers, it was a wakeup call as to just how out of control things were beginning to spiral.

This came to a head in the fall of 1979 when one of the original Atari VCS programmers, Alan Miller, set a meeting with Kassar to discuss a fix for this growing issue. He felt that the programmers weren't being treated fairly for the value they were bringing to the company. He didn't see the work that he did as a simple business transaction, but rather as art, and he wanted it to be treated as such. In more traditional artist contracts, they were given insight to—and rewarded for—sales numbers, which directly affected their pay. He understood that this was different from what they had done up to that point, but felt that, with small teams where they were each directly responsible for such a large part of the game, they deserved better. Miller knew this would be an uphill battle, but he became increasingly frustrated with Kassar's resistance to the idea.

As he worked to get this pushed through, Miller shared the idea with his closest friends at the company—Dave Crane, Larry Kaplan, and Bob Whitehead, all of whom also felt dissatisfied with the current structure. They believed the artist's contract to be a more fair way of compensating them for their hard work, especially as Atari continued to grow at astronomical rates, but they had a hard time seeing it as something that would be immediately implemented. They joined forces and began petitioning for support in their management, which was initially well received but then fell flat, leaving them stuck in a difficult place: they didn't feel valued, but they had nowhere else to go.

Using the internal memo to calculate the direct value they brought to Atari that year, the four men made one final attempt at negotiating with Kassar. They drafted a proposal for their desired contracts that included profit sharing and the ability to take credit for their work, claiming that the four of them had been directly responsible for more than $60 million of Atari's $100 million in VCS software revenue that year, but had received less than $100,000 in compensation. They weren't asking for the world—they weren't naive, and knew that value isn't passed through in full to the creator—but felt there was a common ground more equitable to both parties.

Kassar, unimpressed with their proposal, declined and, according to a 2007 interview with David Crane for *Gamasutra*, told them, "You are no more important to Atari than the person on the assembly line who puts the cartridge in the box." They knew there was nothing left for them at Atari; they could stay, but Kassar's ever-evolving influence over the company had left a bad taste in their mouths, and they knew there had to be something better out there. Crane and Miller left that same year; Kaplan and Whitehead stayed just a bit longer, hoping things would improve.

At the time, Atari was the home console market leader by a long shot, and they knew that going to a competitor would be torture after having the freedoms they had experienced at Atari. They were conflicted. Eventually, Crane and Miller had an idea. What if they didn't have to go work for someone else? What if they could work for themselves, implementing the change they wanted to see in how people were compensated, and still make games for the VCS?

This was completely unheard of at the time, as Atari was the sole provider of games to the platform; the company didn't allow other people to make games for the platform because that would risk cutting into its sales. The idea of third parties had existed with other computer systems, as they were much more open platforms, but never in gaming. If you wanted to compete with Atari, you released your own system. It was risky, but Crane and Miller believed it could be rewarding in a massive way. Plus, they kind of wanted to stick it to Kassar and knew just how to do it.

In October 1979 Crane, Kaplan, Miller, and Whitehead founded Activision; they were quickly funded, setting off to work immediately on their own titles that would run on the VCS platform. This angered Kassar, and he quickly filed a suit against the company claiming that their intimate knowledge of the VCS was property of Atari and that they were wrongfully using it to profit. Atari lost, and Activision went on to release its own games, to much acclaim.

This series of events left many Atari programmers wondering if they had better options, and many of the original programmers from the Bushnell era ended up leaving for other opportunities. They might be making $35,000 at Atari, but other companies would pay them twice that to come make games for them—for many programmers, it just made too much sense to leave. As the market began to open up, they knew they had more options than ever.

For others, the thought of working at Atari was worth the short-term cash loss. Many of them were new programmers who didn't have much experience and knew the opportunity to work there and learn from the best was more valuable than an increase in salary. It was early in their career, and they knew that in an industry so young, knowledge would be key to their long-term success. Besides, the longer you worked at Atari, the more credibility you established in the industry. They clearly believed in the long-term viability, so why not just wait it out?

Plus, they liked the increased competition. With more games releasing every year, the whole field was growing. Sure, there was a chance that their slice of the pie might get smaller, but if another game got someone interested in one of theirs down the road, that seemed like a win. Not only that, but Activision's main mission was to do things that Atari would never have let them do; the programmers weren't exactly sure of what that meant at the time, but they knew that Activision had to do something different if it wanted to beat Atari, and they wanted to be able to counteract that.

Watching from afar as the drama with the Consumer Division and Kassar went down, Atari's Coin-Op programmers knew this was their chance to shine. Theirs was a much smaller team and didn't have to worry about cartridge sales, so while it did bug them a bit that they didn't share in the company's success, they remained mostly unaffected and pushed forward. Though most of 1978–89 had been focused on the VCS, Coin-Op had steadily been putting out new hits like *Asteroids*, *Lunar Lander*, and *Super Breakout* that would take years to replicate for the VCS.

They kept to themselves, remaining true to the focus on entertainment and innovation that Bushnell had set all those years ago. They knew that coin-op gaming would eventually be surpassed by home console gaming as technology advanced and became more cost-efficient, but that didn't stop them from pushing the envelope and continuing to innovate in ways previously not thought possible.

Little did they know that they were just beginning to create what would later come to be known as the golden age of arcade gaming, taking over the hearts and minds of the nation and forming the basis for what would soon become a multibillion-dollar industry.

The First Concept

4

T HE STORY OF *MISSILE COMMAND* IS NO ORDINARY TALE. IT doesn't weave together multiple conflicting perspectives or tell of the time when an idea magically came to its designers during a drug-infused trip to the California desert. It does, however, tell the story of one man who was tasked with creating a simple radar-based game and found a message that haunted him so greatly that he was uncontrollably compelled to share it.

This is the story of *Missile Command*, no doubt, but it is also the story of Dave Theurer, the former Atari programmer who took a simple request asked of him by his bosses and found himself so engrossed in it that it consumed his every thought, haunting him out of the gaming industry and away from the very culture that allowed such a powerful topic to manifest itself within his consciousness. He did not live through a time of tragedy or witness grisly monstrosities; rather, he created them in his head and was engulfed by his own self-obsession with these very creations.

A relatively ordinary man by all accounts, Theurer was a young computer programmer starting off in the still-developing world of video game production. He was fresh out of college and new in the industry, so he didn't have much experience; he needed a chance to stand out and make his mark.

Enter Atari.

We've already covered how this new startup was breaking records and pioneering the early days of the gaming landscape, but let's take a moment to examine the company's surroundings and contextualize this a bit. This was the late 1970s, early 1980s. The world was covered in a shroud of nuclear war. Would it happen? Who knew, but the thought alone was scary enough. No one could be trusted, not even computers. The relationship with technology was tricky at the time, as it was still an emerging phenomenon and, while most could see the benefits to it, some were still wary of the enormous power that it provided. Leading up to this point, computers took up entire silos and controlled most of the world's weapon systems, so there was an inherent fear that came with them as a result.

> Showing just how much distrust there was in welcoming computers into the average American home, Atari was forced to make the Atari Video Computer System with wood-grain paneling on the front to downplay its technical capabilities. People didn't know if they wanted computers in their home yet, so the paneling allowed it to blend in with the home audio and television setups that were common at the time. In doing so, this changed the way most consumers looked at the VCS, transforming it from a computer to a home entertainment device, something they were much more comfortable with.

The average consumers weren't skilled enough to understand how computers worked or why they would really need one, but everyone could understand gaming. We hadn't yet reached the peak of *Pac-Man* fever, but it was beginning to build up as coin-op games became a much more public mainstay through the innovations and culture that Atari was creating with hits like *Pong* and *Space Invaders*. Though these had previously been looked at as nothing more than gimmicks used to pass the time, they started to break through as more people were able to get their hands on them and understand why they were fun. Popularity started to increase, and Atari couldn't order games fast enough. They'd hire a new programmer on and immediately give him or her a game to work on, trying to push new titles out as fast as they could to keep up with the demand.

In 1980, Theurer joined Atari and was immediately put on *Atari Soccer*, a four-player game that followed in the line of Atari's successful sports series. It wasn't groundbreaking, and certainly didn't offer him opportunities to be creative with the idea, but he was a junior programmer and it was his first project, so he didn't really mind. Theurer handled his portion of the development with relative ease, and *Atari Soccer* was released in April 1980, putting him on the hunt for a new project.

Through this arcade craze, Theurer was given the perfect chance to make a name for himself as a junior programmer. Even in those days, a junior programmer would never be given his own game to work on; he'd likely join on as a part of a larger team and just tag along where he could be of assistance. It was an okay path, but it was slow. But because Atari couldn't keep up with demand at the time, Theurer was given the opportunity to own something from start to finish, taking everything into his own hands.

This opportunity came from none other than Gene Lipkin, then president of the Coin-Op Division and vice president of sales at Atari, who had a game he wanted made and needed someone to take it on. Lipkin was a big-time player at Atari, a head honcho for sure, and was ultimately responsible for every game that Atari published in a coin-op cabinet, so when he asked you for something to be made, you started making it regardless of whether you believed in it or not.

One day Lipkin called department head Steve Calfee, Theurer's boss, into his office. This wasn't an unusual occurrence, but Calfee could tell the vibe was different this time as Lipkin sat behind his desk slowly flipping through the pages of a magazine. Turning his attention to Calfee, he flipped the magazine around and pointed powerfully to a story about satellites. In this story, one thing caught Lipkin's eye: a radar screen. "Steve, make me a game like this," Lipkin said.

Oddly enough, no one who was there can recall the contents of the story or whether it was actually a story at all, but perhaps rather one of the terrible ads you see at the back of magazines that make bold claims about the future. Regardless of what it was, it set into motion the initial concept for one of the most influential video games in history.

Having just wrapped *Atari Soccer*, Dave Theurer was free to take on the project and had proven himself more than capable of leading something like this, even if it was a bit of a big ask for someone so new to game development. But to be fair, everyone at Atari was relatively new to game development. Some had been around longer than others, but it wasn't like anyone was sitting on twenty-plus years of experience. They were all new to game programming and were to some degree figuring it out as they went along. Every project was filled with innovation of some kind, whether it was adding color, a new control style, or new mechanics; every game was innovative and this required a bit of luck and a whole lot of experimentation. Calfee saw something in Theurer and gave him a shot to try to make something similar to what Lipkin had asked for.

Calfee called Theurer into his office and gave him the lay of the land. "Gene wants something like this," he said, showing him the magazine cutout. "Think you can do that for me?"

Theurer understood and agreed that he could, officially taking on *Missile Command* as his next project. Well, sort of. What they asked him to make versus what he ended up making weren't exactly on the same page, but we'll get into that later.

At the time it was very common to jump around from game to game, trying to find something that stuck. Atari needed to get as many games out as quickly as possible, so if one wasn't working, programmers often just jumped to another project that seemed likc it was going somewhere. They'd often finish these games, but sometimes they just weren't good enough to put out, so they were scrapped and the programmers moved on. It was almost impossible for programmers to knock things out of the park with their first project, so it was extremely common for them to devote themselves entirely to a project for months, only to move to another project right as they finished and as it became clear that their game would never see the light of day.

At the time, no first-time programmers had their first games published. They worked on them for a bit, learned the ropes, and subsequently moved on to other things. It was well known to Atari employees that this was the case, so for many new programmers, it was a bummer knowing that all their hard work would be for nothing and the game would inevitably be scrapped. This common occurrence was eventually renamed Theurer's Law after *Missile Command*'s release in 1980.

Back then, big games weren't three-year projects worked on by two thousand people like they are today. If the resources were there, they might have allotted a junior programmer to the team to assist, but for the most part, it was just the one programmer handling most of the development process. At this early stage in game development, having multiple programmers on a single project wasn't common practice, if only due to the intricacies of how games were worked on at the time. It wasn't as simple as today ("Simple?" those in game development gasp); there weren't giant servers set up to sync data across an entire team to ensure you were working on the right code base and that it wouldn't all break upon being compiled. It was just a single person working at his or her desk from start to finish, not relying on anyone else to ensure the project was ready for release.

With *Missile Command*, things were different. Theurer might have been one of the newer programmers on the team, but this was direct from the boss, so it was all hands on deck. Even so, "all hands on deck" meant one additional programmer, and he wasn't flush with experience either. Rich Adam, who was also in the initial pitch meeting in Calfee's office, was assigned as Theurer's junior programmer on the project, and the two set sail on making a masterpiece.

I say "set sail" because there's actually a good parallel here between early game development and the discovery of new land. They knew where they were starting and had a rough idea of where they wanted to end up, but getting there was uncharted territory and they were certain to encounter massive challenges along the way.

Theurer and Adam started to pull things together somewhat quickly, but coming up with ideas was one thing; making them happen with the hardware that was available at the time is another.

"Okay, so you've got these missile trails coming in from the top, and you've got these bases at the bottom. The trails are missiles coming in and you shoot missiles up from your bases to intercept them. You try to save your bases," Calfee recalls, sharing what he envisioned from the magazine clipping. That's all they had to go with.

As young designers without a ton of experience, where would they start on a project like that? Luckily there was at least something to go on, and it's not as though the average American had seen a real missile strike, so there was some room for interpretation, but it wasn't the slam dunk they likely thought they were going to score when they signed on. Could they really make that happen in a world of *Pong* clones and slow, simple-action games? They weren't sure, but they were ready to find out—no matter what it took. They were at the forefront of crafting the future of entertainment, and that meant encountering a lot of important questions with difficult, yet-to-be-discovered answers.

Lucky for us, Theurer and the programmers at Atari weren't the type to let a little trial and error get between them and success. In fact, that's how most of their programming went. They'd try something, see how the game reacted, and adjust from there. In modern game development, there's a lot of graphics-based building tools so you know how something is going to turn out before actually running the code; but that wasn't the case at Atari. They were building the graphics engine literally bit by bit.

Lucky for them, Atari wasn't too concerned about it being exactly as they had envisioned. They just wanted it to hit one core beat: nuclear missiles fired from the USSR toward the US, which was defended by the player. That's all they really wanted; everything else about how to make that happen was secondary.

Theurer was shaking with excitement after leaving Calfee's office and could barely contain himself. He finally had a project he was in charge of, and he would finally be able to prove to himself and to others that he could break his losing streak and release his first game to the public. "My spine was tingling," he remembers. "I just had this feeling it was going to be fun."

Fun, yes, but as the excitement subsided, Theurer was starting to realize the gravity of creating something like that in the current political climate and, despite the project being in its infancy, reservations began to bubble up.

Theurer understood the concept of civil duty that Lipkin wanted to instill in players, and he knew how powerful it was to feel that sense of patriotism that came with standing up to defend one's country, but he was worried about his work being used to instigate any of the *less than ideal* manifestations of patriotism that came along with the good. The political climate at the time was dicey; a single mention of any potential claims of communism or anything less than full devotion to the mission of the United States could lead to ostracizing and name-calling, all under the veiled guise of patriotism. Theurer wanted nothing to do with that; he didn't believe in it as a viable approach, and certainly didn't want to give legs to such actions.

Though it wasn't a popular decision and directly contradicted requests from his bosses, he believed that labeling the enemy as the USSR in a hostile role against the United States would come back to haunt Atari, so he pushed back to use a nameless enemy and remove all association with both the United States and the Soviet Union.

Looking back at this now, this one decision had perhaps the most impact of all those made throughout the development— not only for political reasons but also for design implications. Initially, the six cities were listed as Eureka, Los Angeles, San Diego, San Francisco, San Luis Obispo, and Santa Barbara—all major cities in California. Oddly enough, this wasn't for any reason other than just how full of itself Atari was at the time. "Atari headquarters were in California. We were so egocentric that we had the missiles coming across the Pacific aimed directly at us," Rich Adam recalls.

Once they allowed their egos to subside and were able to take a step back to rethink this approach, Theurer and Adam realized just how big of a mistake simply naming the cities would have been from a gameplay perspective. The simple removal of these cities allowed them to take the game in a direction many game developers still haven't been able to recapture to this day: they let the player choose what cities they were, though it wasn't so much a choice as it was a subconscious attachment.

Even with this choice pushing them in the right direction, there was a part of Dave Theurer that still didn't feel right about it. Most games at that time were so basic that they tended to focus on an enemy attacking you, and you killing the enemy to stop him. Theurer didn't like the idea of the player taking any kind of offensive action, even if it was in retaliation.

Just as he had fought to keep any kind of political and potentially jingoistic label on the attacking force, he didn't want the game to be the cause of any kind of incitement, and felt putting the player on offense did just that. If you were simply defending, that's one thing; but you striking back in return was another path that Theurer didn't want to have anything to do with.

In his acceptance of the project, he made it clear that his work on the project was conditional based on two qualifications: (1) there would be no names of countries attached to either the attacking force or the defending force, and (2) the game would be purely defensive and never put players in situations where they would be the aggressors.

In doing this, Theurer ensured that players would retain the sense of patriotism that came with the theoretical service of protecting their country from foreign attack while taking away any notion that retaliation was necessary. He wanted players to be so focused on survival that the thought of striking back never even crossed their minds.

To Theurer, the thought of retaliation didn't fly with the sense of patriotism that he held to. He morally couldn't make a game in such a climate that advocated for the player releasing a counterattack without proper context. He just couldn't do it; it wasn't the kind of person he was.

In his eyes, the purely defensive standpoint preached of a higher calling, a duty—one that, in the end, accomplished the same goal without taking offensive action to escalate the situation any further. You were saving your nation; it didn't matter if there were consequences for the opposing force. It was less about mutually assured destruction and more about doing what you could to aid your country in its greatest hour of need.

He was worried that pairing the touchy political climate with such direct incitement of those very shallow patriotic tendencies could result in players leaving the game with the inverse feeling of what he wanted to portray. He wanted nothing to do with the heightened sense of militarism found in America at the time, and was worried that enabling players to act in opposition would breed a new generation filled with misguided, unstoppably blind patriotism that hurt their fellow Americans who did nothing but share distant genes with those who were now our enemy.

By refusing to give players the opportunity to fire on other countries, especially the USSR, Theurer was instead breeding a new generation of players who strived for alternative methods of survival, however temporary they might be. It wasn't about finding a way to come out on top in a battle, but finding some way to stay alive as long as possible, even if you ultimately lost in the end.

Even if he wasn't fully aware of it at the time, this was Theurer's ultimate challenge. He wasn't just building out an arcade game; he was also attempting to use that game to modify the pervasive mind-set at the time. Landing in the latter years of the Cold War, when things were really coming to a head, this was a brave undertaking, but one that he felt necessary if he was to take on the project.

For Theurer, giving players the opportunity to defend their nation was just as heroic as giving them the option to fight its enemies; it was something they could be just as proud of in the end. This didn't line up with how the rest of the world was thinking at the time and certainly wasn't something you experienced in video games.

The thought of defending one's country wasn't just heroic to Theurer; it was selfless and one of the most moral things someone could do for the country. War is aggressive by nature, but by removing the option to respond to that aggression in kind and instead focusing on protecting oneself, he felt that nothing could be more honorable. It was a noble effort, and he felt that offering players the opportunity to strike back without the context of what leads up to a nuclear attack was the opposite of noble.

"Realizing that these bombs would kill all of the people in a targeted city, I did not want to put the player in a position of being a genocidal maniac," explains Theurer. Only a crazy person would sling nuclear weapons without context, right? That's what Theurer was convinced of, at least. In his heart he felt that putting players in that situation made them no different from the aggressors they were fighting so hard to defeat.

The solution was simple: by giving players direct control over the defense of their own cities, they could take pride in their survival and feel pain in their loss. They had to choose which cities would survive and which would perish, who lived and who died. In *Missile Command*, you can't save all the cities. There is no winning, only surviving for longer than you did before and doing a better job at it. Make no mistake about it; you're going to lose.

Players had only a split second to make a move, a choice that controlled whether someone lived or died. Would they focus all their efforts on protecting one city? Would they try to keep all their cities alive for as long as possible? It was really up to them, and every game was different. In one game players might focus on trying to keep every city alive that they could, while in the next they might let cities fall, as it was easier to defend just one.

This wasn't merely a gameplay strategy, though. It was meant to create an emotional connection between players and what they were experiencing on screen. It associated the players' quest for survival with the building dread of their impending loss. As the game progressed and resources dwindled, it created a deeper and deeper sense of fear in the player, a fear that there was nothing one could do to stop it. It was over, and you had lost. Theurer's goal was ultimately that in this realization players would understand—or at the very least deeply feel—the consequences of what the game was forcing them to do: choose between the death of many or the survival of a few.

This sort of secondary narrative was something that hadn't yet been attempted at the time. In fact, most games hadn't even started to develop a narrative. How could they? At this point in the lifespan of video games, they consisted of a handful of pixels on the screen shoved together to make some semblance of a recognizable figure. We didn't have the ultrarealistic graphics that we've come to expect in games today. Because of this, it was difficult to really get players invested in your story, especially when they were experiencing it one quarter at a time.

In the creation of this narrative, Theurer was one of the earliest narrative pioneers in the beginnings of modern video games, and he accomplished this without saying a single word. He wasn't forceful with his message; it didn't say, "The United States of America is under attack, defend your country with honor," and it certainly didn't say anything about the loss of life occurring in the process. Rather, it let players internalize those conclusions on their own.

Now, let's not get too deep into this without letting it be said that most of the people who played *Missile Command* never even thought about this. They didn't lie awake at night thinking about the people who they weren't able to protect, and the only time they thought about their decisions was in reference to their final score, not the compounding destruction of life associated with it.

This wasn't what the average player wanted from the game, either, especially during this time period. Arcades were an escape from the everyday terrors of reality. Players didn't need despair thrown in their faces. They just wanted to have some fun, and for most, that's exactly what *Missile Command* gave them. It was bright and beautiful, fun and complex. There wasn't a deeper message for them, but its legacy was cemented regardless.

As with all great art, it didn't need to be heavy-handed. You could like it for what it was. Hell, you could like it solely because it was all that was available and you were on your last quarter. It didn't really matter. In the end, Theurer didn't craft the narrative for people to walk away talking about how it made them feel. He wanted them to experience the concept and eventually make the connection to an unrelated futile effort—in this case, nuclear war.

In doing this he unknowingly crafted one of the earliest instances of player-created narrative presented entirely through gameplay where the player was in complete control. This was unique in so many ways, not the least of which was that, as I've mentioned, games barely had any story to begin with, let alone one that the designer had anything to do with. The game wasn't in charge of how your game played out—*you* were. It didn't control whether Santa Clara was the first to go—*you* were. It didn't choose to defend all cities evenly until finally failing—*you* did, developing your own story of how things went down as a result.

How the game ended was all up to you, the player. No matter what you did, you couldn't win, so it was merely a futile decision in order. You might choose to sacrifice one city for the temporary safety of another, only to lose both in the process.

What decision you made was up to you; the only requirement was that you had to make one.

This is what sets *Missile Command* apart. It isn't about the creator, or even the game itself; it's about you, the player, and what you want to do. Through all aspects of the game, it all funnels back to your decisions and the narrative you craft for yourself. You can play the game however you like. Just as you live your life different from how I live mine, the same is true when it comes to the decisions we might make in the game.

In any apocalyptic story, there are always two kinds of people: there's the guy who wants to figure out what happened and get to the bottom of it, and there's the guy who just wants his Twinkies. We all approach situations differently, and that's what makes our stories unique. The sandbox of *Missile Command* allowed this to shine through in each unique play, ensuring that no two stories would ever be the same. You can focus on your heroic patriotism and save the nation; I can ensure my one city in the corner makes it longer than the others.

It's up to the player how to proceed, but in the end—the singular outcome is made clear with the explosive destruction of that final city: THE END. There is no winner. You cannot win. No matter how well you played and what decisions you made, nothing you did made a difference to change the outcome and stop the inevitable. "The End" is a common sign-off for many works of art across all mediums, but in this instance the strong, capitalized font is meant to signal more, to drive home the desecration that comes with nuclear war.

Heavy, right? Especially for an arcade game mostly played by children and teenagers who hadn't fully come to terms with what a war might actually mean. Adults had seen war and knew its terrors firsthand; American adults were coming off a string of wars at the time, and had seen many during the long-standing conflict with the USSR, so for them there was proper context.

For the youth? Not so much. They didn't have to experience the monstrosities of war—heck, most of them probably had never even imagined what war was actually like. There was no draft. It wasn't something you had to think about at the time, especially if the Cold War had been going on for your entire lifetime. For this group of kids, this was their picture of war: nothing happened, there was no fighting, it was all drawn-out mind games that had been going on forever and didn't show any signs of ending soon.

Theurer knew that to get his message across, it couldn't have a heavy hand; it had to be subtle and unobtrusive. He didn't want to force the message on anyone who wasn't willing to hear it. As luck would have it, he was making a video game! Turns out most people don't play games for the social commentary, so he was already off to a great start. He could instead focus his efforts on making the game enjoyable to play, as that's ultimately what would have the largest impact on the reach of his message.

Using games to tell a narrative was still uncharted territory. They were beginning to earn recognition as more than just a waste of time for children, but the general population was still trying to figure out if video games deserved a seat at the table. Thankfully for us, whether they deserved it or not at the time, they were given a shot, and became ingrained as an everyday part of popular culture.

Presented in any other format, *Missile Command* doesn't work—not in that moment in history when it was released, anyway. Books would fall on deaf ears. Movies would be deemed too sensational to apply to our daily life. Games were the perfect medium—subtle and exploratory. It was up to the players to make that connection themselves, but it was also totally cool if they didn't and just wanted to play a video game. It wasn't giving the player a big wink-wink, nudge-nudge the entire time— if you didn't want to see it, you didn't have to. You could just enjoy the gameplay without it being turned into something bigger that might not resonate with every player.

Atari wasn't going to come out publicly spreading the fear of imminent nuclear war; it wasn't going to tell players their patriotism was misplaced. What Atari was going to attempt was to explain the futility of war. That was all a part of the message, but the company didn't say it—the player did. That's where the beauty of *Missile Command* lies. It's always about the player, never the game. It never tells, always shows. It put the onus on the player, attaching real-world consequences and emotions to pixelated cities and explosions in a way never seen before. In many ways, it still hasn't been seen again even now, even decades later.

As these core components of the game's design philosophy began to formulate for Theurer, he realized just how large of an undertaking this would be. Fearing that *Missile Command* had the potential to fall victim to the same fate as the first project of so many other Atari programmers, he was determined to break that streak and release *Missile Command* to the world. He believed in the game concept and the message that he could share. It was a special opportunity, and one that he just couldn't pass up.

Would he end up like everyone else who had felt just as confident at one point or another? We all know that the game came out, but that's not the real story. The real story is how close Theurer came to that very fate, and how it would alter the course of gaming history.

Getting the Green Light

5

THIS ISN'T A TECHNICAL MANUAL FOR *MISSILE COMMAND*. I'M not going to pretend to know how the circuit boards work or how Dave Theurer and Rich Adam accomplished any of the programming feats—I'm not qualified to tell you about any of that and won't insult you by pretending I am. I'm here to tell you about why it matters. But I do think it's important to get into some of the deeper aspects of *Missile Command*'s design to really understand how these impacted the player's experience and reception of the game's narrative.

With such an iconic title in gaming history, it's easy to forget that it went through the same development process as every other game that's been released. There were ups and downs, and things certainly didn't go as planned, but Theurer and Adam eventually worked through it and got it to where it is today—though not without a few bumps and bruises along the way.

But first they had to get the project approved. The order had come down from above to make the game, but that didn't mean they had completely free rein over where they went with it. Calfee trusted them, and was there more to ensure that they had the right executive sign off in case Lipkin or someone from above inquired about the project. He wasn't involved in the day-to-day process, and he sure wasn't going to tell them how to make their game.

After coming to terms with what their concept wasn't going to be, they had to outline what it *was* going to be. This wasn't as easy as it sounds. They had the rough concept they had been given from Lipkin, but there was a ton of gaps that needed to be filled in before they could begin production. If they didn't do it now, it would slow them down during development, and that was the kiss of death. If they were to go about this right and get the game released to arcades, they needed to plan enough to get it moving in the right direction from the start.

They took the guidelines that they were given and fleshed them out into basic concepts—a radar screen, incoming missiles, bases to defend, scoring, and so on—and started to work out how they might actually be implemented. It wasn't as easy as saying, "You're looking at a radar screen filled with incoming missiles. You must fire back to defend your cities." That was the easy part. They needed to work through how it might actually work in an arcade setting.

First they needed to think through what the player might be defending. Knowing they would need multiple missile launch points to fire their defensive missiles from, they chose to have three missile bases, one on each side of the screen and a third in the middle. This would allow players to fire from multiple areas, spacing out the number of missiles they would be able to fire from any one point, curbing abuse. This was a big factor they had to consider in the arcade. With any arcade game, score was the ultimate objective, and players would do their best to find any exploitable mechanic to use to their advantage. Once this mechanic made its way into the wild, there was no going back; your game was done. There weren't patches like there are with current games. It needed to be right when it gets burned to the boards and sent out.

Luckily, these were things that Theurer and Adam found pretty quickly when playing the game for hours on end. Since so much of the process was trial and error when developing, you really had to play the game a lot. You couldn't program these mechanics for a few hours and come back for a quick test game—you really had to get in deep with the game, just as your players would, and find out how they would feel about it. This often meant test plays at the office within their shared lab. Here other game developers at Atari would play the game and offer feedback on what they thought worked and what could be improved.

Though there wasn't a very long development cycle, Theurer was obsessive about testing out every possible outcome that could occur. This meant that he played more *Missile Command* than anyone, really putting in the extra time, even on things that didn't work, to find out why and to tweak things to be better for the player. It's just the way his brain worked.

Once they nailed down the locations of the missile bases, they had to figure out what you were defending. Ultimately, there wasn't really any option other than cities. It was easy to group multiple cities together and give the player something to latch onto. Plus, each city could take a few hits and some parts would still remain, just as if a real city was hit with a missile. But once these cities were implemented, the bottom of the screen became an amorphous blob that all merged together—it wasn't clear what players had to defend and what they didn't. Adam turned to Lyle Rains, Steve Calfee's boss, who had been in the original meeting with Gene Lipkin, for assistance.

Rains quickly solved the conundrum, simply suggesting they elevate the missile bases on mountaintops to have them stand out more. "Why don't you just do it where you have these raised bases on these little mountaintops?" he said. "You have three of those. One left, middle, and right; with cities in between those. Just do that."

He eventually figured out the best way to position it, using Rains as a resource, and that created the basis for Theurer's defensive message. There were rumors of railroads being implemented at one point that would give the player another target to defend, but Adam doesn't recall this being the case, claiming the cities were the main focus for what the player would be tasked with defending.

They even realized that simple missiles wouldn't be enough. Eventually, the player would grow too good and it would cease to be challenging. If there's one thing Theurer wanted most, it was for the game to be a hybrid of challenging and fun. Arcades were filled with games that didn't offer much in the way of competitive play. They were aimed at children, but he wanted to go for the teenager-to-adult demographic. It had to be challenging, and they needed more enemies to make that a reality.

They eventually came up with the idea to add planes and satellites that would fly by, starting at a lower elevation on the screen to give the player less time to react. This required the player to look at multiple places on the screen and have a much better sense of the entire playing field, not just where the missiles were entering from the top of the screen. It was all about the balance. But even then, Theurer didn't think it would be challenging enough.

They decided to make one last addition: multiple independently targetable reentry vehicles (MIRVs), missiles carrying multiple warheads that split off toward different targets after they were launched. These were missiles that would appear to be flying in as a single missile, but would branch off randomly, turning into multiple missiles flying in different directions. Players would need to react quickly to ensure they would get all the stray missiles heading toward different cities on the coastline.

It added a frantic, but fair, element to it that Theurer liked; he was finally starting to feel like the game could hold up against high-level players, offering a drastic increase in difficulty with each ensuing wave of enemy fire.

But he wasn't satisfied. "Yeah, it's fun," he said, trying to figure out what to do next. "It just sort of plateaus, and we need more." He wanted something for the ultra-high-level players, something that, should players make it far enough in the game to see one, would strike them with devastating effect. Then he figured it out. "What if they could avoid your explosion?" he said to Adam, trying to find a mechanic that eventually led to a Game Over.

This is where smart bombs come into play. These weren't your average missiles; they could maneuver around and dodge your defensive missiles. They didn't blindly dive into explosions in the same way that the simple missiles and MIRVs did. Theurer created a way for the missiles to recognize that the flashing color in their current path was a defensive shot and attempt to divert their path. This effectively allowed the smart bombs to see what was in front of them. It didn't always work, obviously, but required much more attention from the player, and made it so they couldn't just spam the top of the screen with defensive missiles. They had to be thorough and meticulous—calculated. This ultimately gave the game the edge it needed to offer players something new each time and to crank up the difficulty as the levels rose, giving it a more timeless nature as it took away the forced ending.

As Theurer and Adam were sorting through all this, they eventually put pen to paper and settled on what would become the basis for everything to come, as is noted in their original pitch:

TO: Steve Calfee
FROM: D. Theurer and Rich Adam
DATE: May 30, 1979

SUBJECT: GAME DESCRIPTION FOR COASTAL DEFENSE
GAME

Possible game titles: "World War III," "Armageddon," "The Edge of Blight."

Object of the game: To save the displayed coast from several waves of in-coming nuclear warhead bearing missiles by blasting them out of the sky with defensive missiles.
Hardware: color monitor, 1 trackball, 3 push (fire) buttons.

Number of players: either a one or two person game. In two person mode, players would take turns defending their coasts. The switch point would be between incoming missile waves.

Display and control description:
The color monitor will display a radar scan view of the coast and the offensive and defensive missile action.

The coast will be displayed across the bottom of the screen. Cities and missile bases will be identified on the coast. Color coding will be used to indicate their status (unattached, damaged, demolished) and importance (large or small population, depleted or full stocked missile base).

The offensive missiles will come down from the top of the screen and go toward the coast, leaving a trail. They will appear as a blip on the monitor as the radar beam scans over them, from left to right. These missiles will attack in waves. Succeeding waves will be more difficult to intercept. Later waves may also contain MIRV type missiles, which break apart into several missiles after a certain length of time. These missiles will be targeted toward a city, missile base or barren area by the computer.

The defensive missiles will rise from the missile bases displayed on the coast and fly to the location on the radar screen requested by the player. There will be 3 missile bases, each one associated with a fire button on the player's console. When a fire button is depressed, a defensive missile will be fired from the associated missile base. Before the beginning of each wave, the missiles in each undamaged base will be restored to a predetermined number.

A cursor will be displayed on the screen and guided by the trackball. When a defensive missile is fired, it will be guided by the computer toward the cursor. A new mobile cursor will appear so other, simultaneous shots can be fired.

When a defensive missile gets to the cursor it explodes, destroying all "close" incoming missiles. If a defensive or offensive missile collides with the coastal area, an explosion will occur. Points will be awarded for effectiveness in defending the cities and missile bases. The score will be displayed at all times, and color-coded status of coastal areas will be updated after any impacts. ABM's [antiballistic missiles] will travel faster than incoming ICBM's [intercontinental ballistic missiles].

Game termination and scoring:
The game will be terminated when a player's 3
missile bases are destroyed or when 2, 3 or 4 attack
waves are done. The number of waves will be option switch selectable for a game, so the destruction of that number of waves will terminate the
game.

Alternatively, if an unlimited number of waves
were given per game, each wave would be more
difficult to intercept. The game would be terminated by the destruction of the player's 3 bases.

The feature allowing entry of player's initials
if his score is in the top 10 will be supported.

Game options:
The appearance of the coast will be customizable
to the area in which it is played to give it local appeal. Coastlines for California, the U.S. East Coast,
Western Europe, and Mediterranean would be
available, possibly as monitor overlays. This option
will depend on available memory.

The number of defensive missiles restocked before each wave could be an operator option.

The number of incoming missile waves, if fixed,
could also be an operator option.

Theurer and Adam outlined the core tenets of the experience, creating what they believed to be the most fun game possible. That's really all they wanted at this point: to give the
player something memorable, and this was unlike anything that
had really been done at the time. Things like smart bombs
hadn't been used in video games; this was an entirely new way
of approaching ramping up a game's difficulty. They didn't just
make things more punishing; they created an enemy that could

dynamically react to the player's actions—just as they would in real life. This was an entirely new technology and one that Theurer and Adam hadn't really anticipated they would need— hence their absence from the initial green-light pitch—but would later come to find as one of the strongest pieces of gameplay at higher levels.

They might not have been the most experienced programmers at Atari when they started on the project, but they knew what they wanted to get from it and were going to do everything in their power to ensure that it ended up as it should for players. They always wanted to do right by players. They might not know how to do something, and it might take them a while to figure out, but they would figure it out—no matter what. That was the culture Atari had developed, and Theurer and Adam thrived on it at the time.

Now that the general gameplay designs were locked, they knew they had to move on to the most important part: How would it all come together, and why should the player care? This was a tough question for them to answer at the time. They felt they were making something fun, and knew that players would eventually think so too, but they needed to get them to drop in that first quarter if they were to have a real effect. They needed the hook and didn't want to rely on other people to give it to them.

As they set to figuring it out, they discovered just how powerful what they were looking to create was. It was a tough time; people often used arcades as an out, an escape. But they saw this as a responsibility to share a powerful message and touch the lives of those living through these struggles. If they really wanted to connect with players and break through in such a critical and vexing time as this, they needed to do something more than just provide them with fun. They had to break through that barrier and transcend beyond that level to something that players could actually associate with, to something that gave them a deeper understanding of the time they were currently in and what effects video games could have on the world at large.

For most people, video games were simply an escape. But for others, they allowed something deeper, a second narrative. It wasn't so much the story of what you were experiencing in the game itself, but rather the experience of you experiencing the game. This kind of connection was unheard of at the time, something that Theurer wasn't sure they were going to be able to pull off, but if you know anything about Theurer by now, you know he was going to try anyway. As he looked to drive that connection home with the player, he struggled with one major question: How?

Finding Meaning in Pixels

6

CREATING AN EMOTIONAL CONNECTION WITH A VIDEO GAME player is no easy task. Creating an emotional connection with someone stepping up to play your game in a crowded bar between beers and slices of pizza? That's even harder. It's loud, they can't hear. They have a quarter and expect it to keep them busy for a few minutes. If you can hook them in those first few minutes, you're golden. If not, they move on. Even if you do win them over, it's temporary. There's no real promise of a lasting connection to the game beyond a simple, "Hey, that was fun."

That's okay, though, because there isn't an implied expectation that either of you deserves that from the other. For most arcade games, this was hit or miss. People didn't really expect much, but they also didn't get much in return. *Missile Command* was different. It looked like a fun, colorful, flashy (if entirely shallow) gaming experience, but when you got into it, you realized it was anything but. It certainly had its share of charming gimmicks, but the mechanics and context inspired hard-core fans right away.

It's easy to look back and attribute this to *Missile Command*'s amazing gameplay, but Atari was putting out dozens of games at the time, and they all seemed pretty fun to the people working on them. Still, there was a major difference that set *Missile Command* apart immediately: while the rest of Atari was cranking out as many games as possible based off any idea that came to mind, *Missile Command* was purpose-built with a very specific vision in mind. It wasn't just made—it was designed and engineered to check certain boxes for players.

Gene Lipkin knew from the very second he laid eyes on the magazine clipping that they could build it into something that people would want to play, if only for the intriguing design. Dave Theurer agreed and knew that if he approached it right, there was a major chance for it to catch fire in arcades. As a relatively new programmer, that's a major opportunity—one that's certain to set you on the right career trajectory should you manage to live up to expectations. He wanted to do this and needed to prove himself. He wanted to create something that was more than just successful; he needed it to go beyond the number of quarters Atari raked in every year from the game and to find an opportunity to create a legacy with players—something that wouldn't dissipate when they ran out of quarters. Theurer wanted to create something that stuck with players and consumed their thoughts even when they weren't playing. He needed to create an emotional connection.

His first step in creating this emotional connection was to give players something to latch onto that related to their personal lives.

Here is the game in a nutshell: There are six cities at the bottom of the screen that the player must defend from the impending missile barrage. As the game progresses and the assault gets more intense, they're destroyed one by one. The player slowly loses them all and the game ends. In the early stages of development, these cities were named after major cities on the California coast. Whether subconsciously or not, programmers Dave Theurer and Rich Adam chose cities that were familiar to them—or at least big enough to help fill out the landscape.

But as they progressed through development, this began to have a negative effect. Each and every day, over and over—the cities they loved faced a dreaded fate as they were blown apart time and time again by nuclear missiles. While it was still just a game to them and it was their choice to name the cities after ones they knew intimately, it began to wear on Theurer and Adam throughout development. As time went on, they began to think about their family and friends in these cities, associating that colorful blast of destruction with the ones they loved the most. They weren't just bundles of pixels anymore, they were starting to feel something about them and associate them with real people they knew. And that hit them closer than they ever imagined it would.

It became too much. With the project being as early and incomplete as it was, they were surprised to find just how much they had internalized this. Then the full realization came through: everyone should feel this way. Through their problem they had found their solution as their own experience with the game had just given them the perfect answer to such a difficult task. Tear away the names and let everyone's self-centeredness take over, subconsciously naming the cities after the ones local to them, and giving them the same experience that Theurer and Adam had gone through. Having these cities appear as such but remain nameless allowed players to face this same internalization. What was previously a set of unfamiliar and, at least to the player, arbitrary cities were now the ones most important to them. They were the cities the players lived in, the cities they grew up in, the cities where they fell in love, the cities where they hoped to one day raise a family. It wasn't make-believe anymore.

It's fair to assume that most players didn't hold this connection to the loss of seventeen pixels on the screen in front of them, but Theurer's message wasn't supposed to be that in-your-face. It was about building the subconscious associations with the narrative of the game that over time helped to resonate with the player.

Before they had even begun working on crafting a true narrative, Theurer had already created one of the most important pieces for the player to grab onto. When missiles struck the city, it wasn't just about the loss of *a life*; it was about *the loss of life* that occurred when that city was evaporated in a cloud of pixels. You're one step closer to needing another quarter, yes, but in the span of a few seconds, millions died, and there was nothing you could do to save them.

It's a heavy message, no doubt, but the meaning from Theurer was direct: nuclear war is a frail endeavor in which we are all affected.

To this point, there hadn't been much in the way of narrative in gaming. In fact, it's safe to say there just hadn't been anything deeper than "kill them before they kill you," which isn't saying much. Atari's designers weren't really focused on building anything other than a fun game that people would dump quarters into, so it's understandable that narrative wouldn't be a massive focus, especially with the state of games at the time. With such primitive graphics, many found it hard to believe that games could be anything other than idle bar entertainment. As with any piece of advanced technology, those who fail to believe in the future usually aren't those who change it. But Theurer believed. However crudely he ended up making it, he was bound to insert some sort of narrative about the dangers of war, even if most players might never notice or take even the least bit of actionable information from it. He wanted to make something that was fun—as do most game designers—but also something that would lead people away from the path of dangerous rhetoric, even if it meant that the overall experience suffered as a result. He was a man of principle, and wouldn't let any measure of fun surpass his need to keep the experience purely defensive and anonymous. To Theurer, this control wasn't just "nice to have"; it was a necessity.

To really understand why this was so important to him, we again need to recall the period in which it was released. *Missile Command* came out at the height of the Cold War—it had been going on for what felt like forever, but that didn't mean that the tension wasn't rising the longer the conflict went unresolved. With every passing day, the question of *when* grew greater than ever before. The dread grew stronger.

This was perfect for *Missile Command*. Without 1980, *Missile Command* wouldn't have become what it eventually did. It needed 1980, and 1980 needed it. Pretend with me for a moment that technology didn't advance, and we were focusing solely on the creation; *Missile Command* wouldn't have become the sensation it did if it was released any earlier or later. It needed that dread—that ultimate sense of despair, doubt, and fear. It needed the tension, needed Ronald Reagan as president. Without this perfect storm of circumstance and culture, *Missile Command* would have been a perfectly serviceable form of entertainment, but would have fallen drastically short of the entertainment legacy that it has since created.

It was the perfect culmination of years of tension that built as Theurer took that fateful first step out of Steve Calfee's office. His mind wouldn't stop racing. He couldn't stop thinking about how to build *Missile Command* into what he wanted. It had been only minutes since he first heard of the idea, but he was already beginning to draft out the core tenets of what the game would become as he walked down the hall and back to his desk.

It may have been a bit obsessive, but this early planning was vital to the cohesive and clear vision of how Theurer would shape the project. His vision began to take form. He started to figure out what would be fun for him, how it might look when programmed into the basic tools he had available to him at the time, and even how the player would control such an experience. With each additional piece coming together, it started to feel closer and closer to a manageable idea.

It was all shaking out a bit different from the magazine clippings Gene Lipkin had showed Calfee, but he didn't care; *Missile Command* was now Theurer's project, and he felt he had the ability to take things in his own direction if it meant the game was better off for it in the end. He was the lead programmer, after all—he was put in charge, and he was going to damn well do what he pleased as a result.

Theurer and his small team quickly found that his goals and ideas were proving to be much stronger than anything found in the magazines, and he committed fully to going about it his own way. He wasn't going to ditch the original idea; he was going to make it his own. Sure, the basics weren't too different. The primary motivator was still for it to be fun, and at no point during the development cycle did he ever dream of changing that, but he had bigger things in mind than something that looked vaguely similar to a radar system. He wanted it to be more than that, and was determined to make it happen.

The fundamentals of the radar design that Lipkin passed along were scrapped, and they moved forward with Theurer's ever growing vision. At the time, they had the authority to do so—Atari was all about the creativity of the individual and doing things on your own until the game was ready to ship. It's not like they had a big team that needed to be checked up on; there were only a few of them. Theurer made the decision to focus more on his direction of the game than the original design, and that was that.

Despite the lofty vision growing more complex by the second, a singular goal remained over all others: to make a fun game. In the end, Theurer had the vision he wanted to get across, but he wasn't going to create something that gave up its fun factor to lecture the player about nuclear war. He knew what business he was in—his primary motivator was to build something that could attract quarters in a fun and unique way. Yet he kept his secondary focus in sight at all times as his true goal began to form: to convey the serious and very personal nature of the devastating events found within the gameplay.

He didn't want to make sacrifices to accomplish this, but at no point was he going to allow fun to trump common sense and the set of morals that he held so dear. There was no compromise here—at least, not for Theurer. If there was, he would be gone.

Missile Command wasn't just going to be fun, but would push the player toward something greater. Theurer really didn't care if they agreed fully with his message, he just wanted to get people thinking—to him, that was the ultimate reward. He wanted to change their mind-set. Placing the player in a fully defensive role changed the attitude that most players approached games with. It didn't put them in the situation where the game did something to the player and the player's reaction adversely affected the enemy in return. Instead, Theurer focused on creating a game that never reacted to the player. You weren't able to shoot out the enemy's missile launchers, and you certainly weren't able to kill the enemy to make it easier on yourself. You had to focus solely on yourself and your actions. In doing so, he created a feedback loop based solely on the game's actions, not the player's. It was all about what the game did to the player, not what the player did back. In the end, there's nothing players could really do to stop the game, so why let it affect the incoming barrage? Nothing the player could do would end the onslaught; it could only delay it. The game was still going to execute its plan appropriately. In retrospect, it's like *The Terminator*—but without the change of heart at the end of the film.

Because of this, it was actually extremely common for players to not really understand the game's ending at first. This was partially due to current design convention in which many games didn't have endings, you just lost and that was it, but it was also due to the game's mechanics being similar enough that you didn't really understand the difference in the intent behind the game. It wasn't like most games, where you didn't kill all the enemies and eventually they came back to overwhelm you; it was focused more on your ability (or inability) to protect yourself and the consequences associated with failure.

Most games—including *Missile Command*, as far as the general public was concerned—were all about scores. The higher the score, the better you did, regardless of how far you actually got in the game. This method of play incentivized a ton of different strategies. You might try to keep all of your cities alive for as long as possible, knowing you won't get as far in the end, but that the bonus for each city reaching the next barrage might outpace where you could make it if you let some get by to focus on defending fewer targets. It was really up to you how you wanted to go about it—the outcome was always the same, so it was more about the journey than the destination.

Being unable to fire defensively at your attacker leaves you unable to change the course of action. Instead, you must focus on doing all you can to stop it, even if you know it's nothing but a futile endeavor with a singular outcome. You must change up your city strategy, giving up one city to ensure the survival of the others. Regardless of the impending outcome, you have to give it a shot.

Theurer's hope was that if players knew there was no way to win, only delayed loss, there would be a change in the feeling associated with their role, from one of heroism to one burdened with immense pressure and responsibility. He wasn't trying to mess with players' heads, but instead to get them to think about the consequences associated with such actions, however digital or make-believe they might be. He wanted them to realize through this emotional connection that they could no longer be the hero—they could try their best but would never succeed. He wanted them to feel the responsibility that comes with such power: players could be put in a place where they're expected to save the cities from destruction, only to realize that they're ultimately responsible for those cities' demise.

This was purposeful role assignment by Theurer, designed with hard-core players in mind. He knew that the average players of *Missile Command* were just trying to pass the time with their after-work softball league buddies, not suffer an existential crisis. He wanted this small subset of players to understand the role they were assigned in this situation—a role in which all hope relied solely on them and their ability to defend the cities that looked to them for saving. They were the only ones who could do anything; the pressure was on. If they weren't able to defend their cities from attack, that was it. There was no one else who could do it.

As we know, they weren't able to defend their cities in the end. Even still, winning wasn't really the point. Theurer wanted players to embrace the absolute dread that their role required. It didn't really matter that they couldn't defend their cities; it was no black mark on their skill record, because there was no one else who could fully defend them, either. It was truly an unwinnable battle, no matter how good at the game players got.

Theurer wanted them to encounter this invisible boundary, one that would force them to think of the cities—and the people contained within them—as more than just numbers. If you play *Missile Command*, you'll notice there aren't numbers assigned to the cities; again, the anonymity encourages players to internalize these cities and make them their own. Once players come to terms with the fact that they can't win, they start to make choices to deter the destruction and stay alive as long as they can. As such, these choices must be rationalized, and this is where things start to get a bit more personal. Forcing players to choose between one group of people and another puts them in a position of power where they're making life-or-death decisions that have real and direct consequences on the endgame.

This position of power is important as the player's role shifts from that of the cities' heroic protector to their failed defender. With nothing to show for your efforts but six craters and pure dread, you're placed in a situation where a new best possible outcome is found. It might not be about winning; it might be about getting as far as you can and seeing where things shake out. As long as you're improving, you're winning, and that's something that pervaded the collective consciousness within gaming arcades at the time. It wasn't ever necessarily about hitting the end screen; sometimes it was just about scoring higher than your friend as you're playing. In a way, it removed heroism from the equation, diverging from the typical hero's journey that we've grown accustomed to in gaming since then. There was no rescuing Princess Peach from the evil Bowser. You weren't able to save them—no matter what, you still lost.

We aren't all able to be John McClane in *Die Hard*; some of us end up shot and used as an elevator prop to send a message. We can't all be the action movie star who saves everything in the nick of time. It doesn't always work like that, and Theurer's main goal was to remind players of the futility of war in hopes that they would relate their gameplay experience to the potential situation we might find ourselves in one day. He wanted them to feel the ups and downs of the gameplay, wanted it to be something that players thought about long after they were done playing. He wanted them to not only feel these deep and wild feelings, but to internalize them to their own personal hopes and fears. He wanted *Missile Command* to be something that people saw not just as a game, but as a true message, the sort of message that only art can provide.

As it turns out, this was extremely difficult. Even reading this, you're probably rolling your eyes, thinking, "Okay, buddy, let's bring it down a notch. It's a video game! No one is weeping about how *Missile Command* subjected him to the horrors of war." Yet as his team got deeper and deeper into the development, Theurer kept pushing for this to be the main message. He knew it would resonate with some and, in his eyes, it only took one person to write a column or share her thoughts with friends to spread the message.

Little did Adam know, Theurer didn't just have a strong feeling about this, he was experiencing this sensation himself; he was beginning to become overwhelmed with the messages found within the game. With the long hours that were common at Atari at the time, the pressure mounting on him to not fall prey to the same curse that had struck down so many first-time programming leads before him, and the intense subject matter at hand, Theurer began to find himself questioning whether it was a step too far. It was a video game meant for teenagers, after all. Maybe the message was too heavy, he thought. But time and time again, he convinced himself otherwise, pressing forward toward release.

"It's not that bad," he told himself, but as he lay down to sleep, he knew the horror that awaited him.

Failure to Innovate
Was Anti-Atari

7

GAME DEVELOPMENT ISN'T EASY. IT'S A LOT OF LATE NIGHTS, caffeine, and head-scratching conundrums that seem so simple once they're solved but prior to that leave you confused for days on end. Everything you're doing is new. The industry centers around technology that's changing all the time—around the drive to be the most technologically advanced, even if it lasts only for a moment.

In the video gaming industry, there's a summit named D.I.C.E. that stands for Design, Innovate, Communicate, Entertain—and that's exactly what games are meant to do. At the crux of any basic game design, you want to tackle these four pillars, typically using innovation to drive the other three. This is why game design is so difficult: you're essentially reinventing the wheel with each new release. If you weren't, you'd be behind, and that doesn't work in gaming. Failure to innovate is a death sentence when you're dealing with such an intense community that's so used to constant progress. Always forward, never backward.

At the time *Missile Command* was being developed, there wasn't a long history of development that you could look back on for lessons. Instead, you were history in the making, pushing things through as you saw fit and creating those lessons for future generations to come. There were no experienced game developers. Games had truly only been around for a few years, and most developers were using trial and error, making things up as they went. If you were stuck on something and didn't know how to fix it, you either asked those around you—if you were lucky enough to be at Atari, where the world's best developers were located at the time—or just kept trying things until something worked or you gave up on it, resigned to the fact that it wouldn't be included.

There are a million little details and a million more ways that these details won't work together. Ten things might work together well, but the addition of just one more can break them all; that's just how it was. There isn't much you can do. Games are hard to make and even harder to actually finish. For Dave Theurer and Rich Adam, this was difficult and frustrating, especially as relatively junior programmers. They knew it was the nature of the beast, but that didn't cut down on the mounting stress that Theurer began to experience as their deadline for *Missile Command* loomed closer with each passing day.

There were some good sides to this predicament too, though. Because there was no standard operating procedure, you had the freedom to experiment and do things your own way. You didn't have to follow standard convention, and you certainly didn't have to answer to anyone else on the team—because there wasn't anyone. It was up to you to decide how to go about things, and because of that, gamers were gifted with a lot of experimental ideas that likely never would have seen the light of day had they gone through committee review.

One aspect of this design was the inclusion of a trackball. At this point in time, trackballs weren't very popular for mainstream applications, especially gaming. They'd seen use in the military, having been designed by the Royal Canadian Navy in the 1950s out of small four-and-a-half-inch bowling balls, but they still weren't common in modern computing appliances, as navigation was primarily accomplished with the strokes on a keyboard.

But in 1978 Atari first decided to use a trackball in *Atari Football*, its breakout arcade hit. Trackballs could stand up to the battering that cabinets took in popular arcades while also offering players greater precision than traditional arcade sticks. Given their military applications and the initial proposal for the game to mimic a radar screen, it only makes sense that Theurer would attempt to include this instead of the traditional—and slow—joystick.

The trackball was visually striking and gave the game an edge to it that drew players in as they passed by. The cabinet's design was already intensely unique, with massive missile clouds filling the entire side of the cabinet launching off to an unknown destination, but the inclusion of the trackball often attracted players who simply wanted to see how it worked.

The trackball afforded the player a much more responsive and reactive level of control, allowing the game to move at a much faster pace than most other games at the time. This would later become one of *Missile Control*'s most defining features, and it caused decades of controversy and confusion as Atari was still figuring out the best way for it to be used at the time of release.

Though trackballs—and their right-side-up computer mouse counterparts—later became ubiquitous with home computing platforms and have been common in dozens of arcade titles since, *Missile Command* was one of the first to take a massive risk by replacing the most common control method with something that was relatively unproven and somewhat confusing to first-time players. If you didn't know any better, it seemed loose, wild, and impossible to control. As more time was spent with it, it became clear that it didn't require the same exaggerated movements of classic arcade joysticks and worked best when given finessed touches. It turned out to be a massive success, showing that with great risk came great reward, even in an era when risk and errors were unacceptable. It had been done before, but no one remembers *Atari Football*; they remember *Missile Command*.

Another defining feature at the time was that the game was multicolored. While it may sound primitive now, the first releases that Atari put out weren't in color; *Pong*, for instance, was entirely in black and white. Using multiple colors was an advanced technology, one that Atari was trying to figure out how best to accomplish with the limited hardware it had at the time. With each advance in hardware, the costs soared. Just to add color, you were looking at replacing multiple parts with more expensive, state-of-the-art upgrades.

Theurer and Adam knew it had to be done, though. The graphics were just too striking to be seen in black and white—they needed color. The game needed to feel *real*. Though the Atari 2600 version later moved the setting to a fictional alien planet far away from Earth, Theurer wanted the colors to remind players of what they were defending, using earth tones that hadn't been seen in games before.

Missile Command wasn't the first multicolor game, despite what some think (at least not according to Adam), but it was the first color game done by Atari, which is where much of the confusion stems from, as many tended to conflate the two due to Atari's strong dominance during this era. This was a huge advantage for Atari at the time, as most consumers hadn't seen anything like it before. *Missile Command* would pull people from the other side of the arcade simply due to the color graphics—they stood out that much.

Oddly enough, it wasn't a massive revelation from the start

that they were going to be able to do it in color. They just did it. During this time, they were unstoppable. Whatever Theurer and Adam wanted to do, they just made happen—and the same was true for the addition of color graphics. They didn't need to be the first ones to do it, they just wanted to do it, and the industry was so new that few had before; so they had to figure out how to make it a reality.

Adam recalls that game developers "didn't know how lucky they truly were, because at that point, you could say, 'Let's make a game about *this*' and at that point, it had never been done, because almost nothing had ever been done." It was an age of exploration. You didn't have to worry about putting out the same thing as anyone else because there weren't other people really making games. You'd just come up with an idea and make it a reality.

This was the same with color. Theurer and Adam just thought, "What if we do this?" and made it happen. When they first got new things working, it wasn't uncommon for them to show them to others around the office to get their opinion on where they were at. With color, the reactions were all the same: "Oh my God, that's color!" It was something that people hadn't seen before. It truly was an inspiring sight at the time, and they were, by their own admission, lucky to be able to bring that experience to consumers for the first time, even if it lost its novelty during development.

After a few months, the novelty did indeed begin to wear off. They had difficulties getting the hardware to work and were looking at it twelve hours a day; it became the new normal. Thankfully, they had the consumers to remind them just how unique it was every time a new player saw it for the first time.

"Oh my God, that's color!"

Ah, there it is.

The trackball and color were just two pieces of what made

Missile Command special, but they formed the basis for what Theurer and Adam had intended all along. They wanted to create something special for players, something that felt nothing like any other game they had played before. In doing so, Theurer and Adam gave people yet another reason to play their game when they might have otherwise ignored it. In an effort to make it as fun as possible and get his message heard by as many people as possible, Theurer pushed the envelope in a way that perfectly encapsulated the conditions they found themselves in: if you thought it, you did it.

Make it happen and change the world.

When Passion Turns to Obsession

8

I N THE DAYS THAT DAVE THEURER WAS BEGINNING TO DEVELOP *Missile Command* at Atari, there was an all-too-common scenario called the Atari Trap, which was the exact manifestation of the work that was described earlier: full devotion to making the best game you possibly could and the long, endless nights required to make that a reality. In a company focused on getting out as many hits as possible, this was extremely common as developers spent sleepless nights finding the best ways to make their game enjoyable in the shortest amount of time. Release good games, and do it often.

Theurer was an unusual case. He poured his heart and soul into the project, but from the very beginning, he stressed the value of a work-life balance. He was fine spending long nights on the project in order to get something done, but he never wanted this to become the norm and worked hard to make that a reality. In the beginning of the project, this was quite easy, despite his overwhelming excitement for what the game could become. He was able to go home on time and create a healthy sense of balance between work and the rest of his life. But as he progressed in development and the game's grip on him grew tighter and tighter, he wasn't able to put up as much of a fight. He tried to avoid it, but like many others before him, he fell prey to the trap and allowed the project to consume and dominate his time.

Before *Missile Command*, most of these projects at Atari were one-man shows. There was only a single programmer on most projects who was in charge of both design and the actual code implementations. This programmer worked with engineers and other team members when necessary, but it still wasn't common to have a big team—you were expected to be able to do most of it on your own. But with *Missile Command* being such a big project, Theurer was given a junior programmer to help with some of the coding. Enter Rich Adam.

Adam was the perfect equalizer to Theurer. For every time that Theurer brought up the greater implications of the game to players, Adam focused on the fun of it all. For every time Theurer said it was about sending a greater message, Adam said enjoyment was the only metric. For some this may seem like the most tumultuous of relationships, but for them it was a balance of yin and yang. They were each other's counterbalances, and they liked it that way.

This changed the dynamic at play between the two of them, especially when it came to their working relationship. They hadn't worked together before, and it was a learning experience from the get-go. Most programmers at Atari were used to doing things on their own. They hadn't ever had to answer to anyone but themselves, and *maybe* their bosses, but most of the times bosses were pretty hands-off once someone had started on a project. As long as you hit your deadline, you were good to go—and even then, they called the shots, so it didn't really matter.

This was different with *Missile Command*; not just with Adam having to report to Theurer as his senior manager, but in Theurer doing right by Adam. With all the eyes on the project, he knew it wasn't just about him, but that they needed to work with each other to succeed.

One of the main reasons that Adam was brought in was to ensure they met a strict manufacturing deadline. Atari had become such a commercial success that it felt a need to create its own manufacturing facility down the road from the Moffett Park offices. With only eight releases in 1979, the manufacturing facility was effectively on standby, waiting for programmers to get the green light that their projects were ready to go. Because of this, there was a very real need for Theurer and Adam to hit the relatively tight deadline imposed on them by Steve Calfee.

These workers were just waiting around for games to come in. There was only so much work they could do ahead of the game coming in or finalizing design work. "[The workers] needed games to manufacture," recalls Adam. "They needed the designs for the cabinets we were going to build and ship." You could only predesign cabinets to a certain extent, as the game teams often found themselves coming up with new and unique cabinet designs to stand out in the arcades, which were quickly becoming crowded with dozens of other fun games. They needed to stand out. But because of this, the workers were stuck, and their team began feeling the heat on ensuring they didn't encounter any delays. With this being their first project together, Theurer and Adam knew they didn't have the luxury of being able to mess this up.

Not only did they need the cabinets built and ready to go, but they had to manufacture the circuit boards, often referred to as ROMs (for "read-only memory"), that the game would live on—and this was the big one. The sheer scale of the project exposed Adam to a new level of pressure he had never experienced before. If you made a mistake and didn't catch it before sending it off to manufacturing, that mistake was present on hundreds of thousands of ROMs. You had two options: leave it, or fix it—and fixing it wasn't cheap. In fact, the additional manufacturing cost to fix something was deemed an unallowable expense, one they couldn't afford to run into. You had to get it right the first time—and fast.

Theurer and Adam grouped up and set off to work on the game, eliminating core elements of the original pitch in order to land on a design that focused on fun above all else. They cut out suggestions from Steve Calfee and Gene Lipkin, focusing on finding alternatives to the problems they were being asked to solve with this design. At the time, it didn't seem crazy—just work, like any other project. There's a strong inclination in successful creators to look back on their creation as if it was a perfectly executed plan of success. In reality, it doesn't always play out that way—it can just feel like work that ends up being really good. That's exactly what *Missile Command* was to Theurer and Adam. That's not to say they weren't excited; they clearly were, but there had been dozens of titles before that Atari programmers thought would be fun that had never seen the light of day.

For Adam, it was no different from every other game he'd worked on. "Everybody thinks of that as 'the golden age,' but to us it wasn't," he remembers. "We were just working and making stuff." To Adam, it didn't feel like a revolutionary time—it was just work. It was something special they were proud to be making, but they didn't spend their days thinking, "Man, these are special times that we're going to look back on fondly as the birthplace of gaming narrative." It was nothing like that—at least not for Adam.

Theurer was a bit different. He knew it was special. It wasn't just a game to him. It wasn't like other projects he had worked on previously. It was a unique opportunity to make a game that was extremely engaging but also carried an important message. This message was one of hope, hope that one could somehow keep this nuclear nightmare from becoming reality. And for Theurer, there was hope, deep down, that he could somehow in-

Dave Theurer standing in front of the newspaper photo from his hit-and-run assistance.
(Credit: Game Developers Conference)

Dave Theurer accepts his Pioneer Award at the 2012 Game Developers Conference in San Francisco, CA.   (Credit: Game Developers Conference)

Atari founder Nolan Bushnell in Madrid, Spain.   (Credit: Javier Candeira)

Nolan Bushnell signs an original Atari 2600 at Campus Party Mexico in 2013.

(Credit: Campus Party Mexico)

Pac-Man corner at Funspot Family Fun Center in New Hampshire.

(Credit: @AzyxA on Instagram)

The reflective *Missile Command* marquee at Funspot Family Fun Center, where
Tony Temple achieved his high score. (Credit: @AzyxA on Instagram)

The front of the original Atari VCS
wood grain home console. As it was
the first time people were being
asked to add video games to their
home décor, Atari wanted it to blend
with common home entertainment
setups of the period.

(Credit: Moparx.com)

An original *Pong* home console
at the Henry Ford Museum in
Dearborn, Michigan.
(Credit: Mark Cameron)

Al Alcorn with Ralph Baer at the 2008 Game Developers Conference in San Francisco, CA. (Credit: Alex Handy)

Computer Space and *Pong*, side by side, at the Museum of the Moving Image in Queens, NY. (Credit: Mel Boysen)

Missile Command Tournament Settings World Champion, Tony Temple, alongside his personal *Missile Command* cabinet at his home in the UK.   (Credit: Tony Temple)

ABOVE: The artwork on the arcade cabinet marquee of *Tempest*, inspired by Dave Theurer's nightmares as a child.   (Credit: Mene Teke)

LEFT: A custom neon Atari sign adorns the walls of Dogs 'n' Dough, which features an amazing selection of retro arcade classics, in the heart of Manchester, England. (Credit: Mark Webster)

A *Missile Command* display at the Game Masters exhibit in Halmstad, Sweden, that showcased the most impactful games in video game history.

(Credit: Retro-Video-Gaming.com)

The well-used control panel of the *Missile Command* cabinet on display at the Game Masters exhibit in Halmstad, Sweden.

(Credit: Retro-Video-Gaming.com)

An excavated copy of Atari's *E.T. The Extra-Terrestrial* that was the subject of a massive urban legend, finally confirmed in the 2014 excavation of the suspected desert dump site.

(Credit: Ed Martinez)

Ted Dabney, Nolan Bushnell, and Al Alcorn with the original *Pong* cabinet.
(Credit: Nolan Bushnell)

Author Alex Rubens posing with a *Missile Command* machine at his wedding in
June 2018. (Credit: Ivy Reynolds)

fluence players and change their perception, showing them what a massive error it was to assume war was the only way. His vision was much deeper than creating an entertaining game; he wanted to craft a meaningful legacy with it, something that no game had truly accomplished to that point. People had really liked *Pong*, and still do to this day, but that's a different kind of legacy than what Theurer was hoping to accomplish. He didn't want *Missile Command* to be around in forty years solely for its gameplay merits. He wanted its effect to be more powerful.

As they progressed further into development, Theurer started to fall deeper and deeper into this goal, subtly pushing the development down that path, all unbeknownst to Adam. While Adam thought they were beginning to make good progress on the game they'd been working on for a few weeks at this point, Theurer was finding himself consumed by the fear-stricken worry he was attempting to induce in the player.

It had only been weeks, but the very thought of what they were trying to get across had already taken its hold on Theurer. Adam? Not so much. Sure, people are different and react to things in different ways. But how could one member of the team be drawn to such a powerful narrative while the other was left completely unaffected?

Oddly enough, this was the end goal with *Missile Command* all along. Theurer knew that they would never get their message across to everyone who played the game, and that 99 percent of players would never think more deeply about what they were playing, but it was a mission for him nonetheless.

If you ask Adam why Theurer was so driven to get this message across, it has to do with his heroic qualities that, more than thirty years after they worked together, still stand out to Adam as unique. Adam saw him as an "incredibly ethical and honest person" who just gave off this superhero "good guy" vibe that was undeniable. In the same way that Superman feels compelled to save those in distress, Theurer carried with him an air that he could always be of help—that there was always something for him to be doing to make his world a better place. And that was true for all facets of his life, not just his work on *Missile Command*. It wasn't just evident to Adam that these qualities existed within Theurer; it was clear in the way Theurer went about his life.

In 1983, three years after the release of *Missile Command*, Theurer was driving his Porsche 928 to watch a fireworks celebration at Moffett Field, a local joint civil-military airport located between Mountain View and Sunnyvale in Santa Clara County, California, when the unthinkable happened. Right in front of his eyes, he watched as a car plowed into a teenage pedestrian and took off. He stopped to help the injured pedestrian and, once he had ensured that other passersby could assist, got back into his car to chase down the hit-and-run driver. He turned onto I-280, putting the 234 horsepower, 4.7 liter V8 to use, racing down the freeway after the fleeing driver. He caught up to him, forcing him to pull over. He was then somehow able to convince the driver to turn himself in and assisted in returning him to the scene, where he was arrested on charges of felony hit-and-run, drunk driving, giving false information to a police officer, and driving without a license. The teenager who had been hit by the driver ended up being paralyzed from the waist down from the collision, and the police said that had Theurer not chased down the driver and convinced him to return to the scene, they most likely would never have caught him.

That's the type of person Dave Theurer is. He risked his own life to chase down a hit-and-run suspect who had clearly shown no regard for human life and brought him to justice simply because *it was the right thing to do*. To Theurer, this wasn't a heroic act; it's just what you do—it's your duty, your responsibility as a human being. That is obviously an extreme example of Theurer's heroic nature, but for those who knew him, it was just one act of many that exemplified his character.

Because of his selfless, proactive nature, Theurer felt compelled to do what he thought was right and do his part in making the world a better place. As work on *Missile Command* progressed and their deadline drew nearer with each passing day, his commitment to finishing it began to consume his every thought.

Would they finish the game in time? Would it be fun? Would it sell? Would anyone understand the message he was trying to impart? Was the message important enough for others? Would the player actually learn anything from it? Was this the right medium with which to impart the message? Would the game create a lasting legacy with the player that went beyond the simple insertion of a quarter into a coin slot?

These were the questions that drove Dave Theurer, and as they circulated in his head, they began to transform from the standard questions that one asks oneself when working on a creative endeavor to an obsession that he couldn't erase from his mind, pushing him to a place he never expected to be at while working on an arcade game. It became less about the business implications of whether they could meet the deadline and people would play the game, and more about the art that Theurer was looking to create.

As this obsession increased and began to consume more and more of his thoughts, Theurer began to worry that he was going down a bad path. But he knew it would be over soon, and he didn't want to burden anyone; he was, after all, a problem solver, not a problem haver. It was in his nature to keep it to himself, and that's exactly what he did. He didn't speak much about it to Adam or anyone else, but, as Theurer recalls, the further they progressed in development, the "more stressed and obsessed with trying to finish" the game he became.

As his brain entered this state of obsession, the destructive nature of the game began to take hold on a deeper level than Theurer had ever imagined possible. It's well documented that creators can often have very tumultuous relationships with their creations: they love what they're working on, but hate the way the need to make it perfect consumes their very being. Some don't know when to stop working or when "good enough" is really good enough. There are too many long nights at the office and broken relationships as they struggle to please everyone while simultaneously pleasing no one—not even themselves. This is an extremely common tendency in high-performing creative people. It's also extremely destructive. Most of the time such people reach their breaking point. It becomes too much to handle and they aren't able to balance everything they need to retain a semblance of completeness.

The breaking point is different for everyone, as is the path to that point, but the process is a result of wanting your creation to be just right—that perfect blend that accomplishes what you want it to for all people. Theurer had a message he hoped to share, but for that to work successfully, he had to ensure that the game was also perfect for people who would never absorb that message. He didn't want to force anything and, despite his defensive approach being a prerequisite to making the game, he knew it needed to be captivating or no one would ever care enough to experience it.

As he worked to make all these pieces fit together, in an attempt to answer all the questions he couldn't shake off, he began to spend every waking hour in his Atari office. He wanted the game to be just right, but with this obsession, he began to encounter fatigue as he watched city after city destroyed by nuclear war. These visions escaped the game world and seeped into his conscience. He began to experience exactly what he had hoped players would feel, which, while oddly satisfying, left him in a place he would never return to again.

Melting Flesh

9

"**A**LL-CONSUMING PASSION."

This was the one phrase Dave Theurer used to describe his work on *Missile Command*. He didn't care what anyone else wanted; he had already deviated so drastically from what Steve Calfee and Gene Lipkin had initially proposed that he didn't really care to hear input from anyone else. He wanted the game to be both appealing and smart—those were his two requirements. He wasn't going to stop working on the project until he felt that both of those requirements were satisfied to the best of his ability, even if he lost a bit of himself in the process.

Theurer takes his work very seriously—even if it's "just a game." He's a creative person at heart, even if games aren't entirely creative endeavors. If he's going to do something, he's going to work at it until it's unequivocally right in his eyes. There isn't another option—there is nothing less than 100 percent perfection for him.

He was absorbed by these thoughts. "Missiles armed with atomic warheads are weapons of mass destruction and one should be deeply affected by their use," he explains. In his eyes, the commonplace acceptance of these missiles in everyday life had minimized their shock factor. Use of these missiles would have life-altering effects for everyone, not just the people under attack. He wanted to bring this notion back to the forefront of our thoughts when the topic arose.

Theurer wasn't alone in the gravity of this feeling either. After realizing the incredibly dangerous position the world was in due to the invention of the atomic bomb, many notable politicians and scientists spoke out about how deeply this issue troubled them—most notably Nikita Khrushchev, head of the Soviet Union until 1964, and J. Robert Oppenheimer, the lead Manhattan Project scientist and the so-called father of the atomic bomb.

The fact that those who were so closely tied to the bomb's development and rise were scared enough to speak out against it deeply affected Theurer. He knew that he could no longer blindly be a part of a culture that perpetuated this as the new norm, a norm in which nations were racing to grow the largest stockpile of these weapons, "just in case." He understood their purpose was more defensive than offensive, just as he had forced *Missile Command* to be, but the prospect of mutually assured destruction left him uneasy.

It was heavy stuff, and it scared the hell out of him. He didn't enjoy that feeling (who would?) but the Cold War didn't show any signs of abating anytime soon, so he wasn't confident relief would ever come. Hysteria was at an all-time high. Everywhere you went, war was at the forefront of America's mind. Go see a movie: nuclear war. Turn on the TV: nuclear war. Watch a speech by President Ronald Reagan: the Strategic Defense Initiative ("Star Wars"), defending us from nuclear war.

Dave Theurer went to work every day, spending hours on a game that carried these same heavy themes. He didn't have the escapes that everyone else did. In fact, it was the opposite. The general public was exposed to generalities and hypotheticals, but Theurer had to watch nuclear war play out on his screen over and over again. Rather than let real-world fears consume him, he buried himself in *Missile Command*, doing what he could to get his project out, doing his part to spread pleasure and excitement in a time of fear. In doing so, he poured every bit of himself and every waking hour of his day into the game. He often found himself staying at the office for days at a time, hiding the fact that he wasn't going home from his coworkers, who would have undoubtedly been worried and concerned by his growing obsession. *Missile Command* became his life, and he was determined to see it through, first-game curse be damned.

In the early days of the project, Theurer sunk everything he had into development. It was his singular goal, both personally and professionally, like an Olympian training to compete. It consumed him. "[The game] is all I think about, almost exclusively," he says. It was his obsession, his singular focus—but he didn't see it that way; he was just working on the project, and it worked for him.

Theurer worked a bit differently from the way most designers did at Atari. Most designers would sketch out as many different gameplay scenarios as they could for any given concept, pick the best one, and build it. Theurer built them all to find out which one actually played the best, chose that one, and worked on it until he came to another fork in the road, and then he repeated the process. This had always been his style, even when he was just learning. With teams this small that typically relied on the decision of their lead designer/programmer, he found this to be a critical part of finding out how to make the best game possible. They hadn't been game designers for very long, so he knew there were always better ways to do things, but often these weren't discovered until they played out every scenario. In doing so he was able to constantly find the best way to approach each mechanic, but this obsessive style of experimentation also opened his mind up to endless thoughts of different styles of death and destruction. His focus on making the game as enjoyable as possible turned to an obsession engulfed in nuclear war.

"I imagined the missiles streaking in, imagined the explosions, but with sounds and visuals, over and over, day after day, until they felt just right," he explains. He didn't just want it to feel right in the moment; he wanted it to feel right while fitting in with the game's tone stylistically. He didn't just want something to succeed in isolation; he needed it to feel like a complete package if his message was ever to resonate with players.

This constant pursuit of perfection left him overworking his mind and body to their breaking points, and *Missile Command*'s potent premise began to take hold in his subconscious. It was no longer just a game. In his mind, parts of it seemed entirely real. Those detailed scenarios that he had envisioned when deciding which to pursue now felt real. They filled his every thought, leaving the pixelated world and entering his personal world. These thoughts soon became dreams, and these dreams soon became nightmares.

ONE EARLY MORNING Theurer is up in the mountains above Silicon Valley. He is getting in a hike, finding it to be the perfect start to the day before heading into the office, when suddenly, he hears a roar from above. He raises his head to the sky to get a better look at what made the noise. "It must have been a jet from Moffett Field," he thinks to himself, but as he turns, he realizes it's moving much too fast. The missile becomes clear to him just as it impacts the city below, sending out a shockwave of heat and dust, obliterating everyone within miles of the impact. Millions are vaporized instantly. As the fireball grows into a mushroom cloud, he feels the air getting warmer and warmer, but he can't move—he is frozen, gazing at the horror before him.

The heat wave overtakes Theurer, jolting him awake. He lies in bed, covered in sweat, horrified at what he's just seen. But there's no time for him to reflect on what he's just experienced; he needs to get back to *Missile Command*, so he gets up and readies himself for his workday.

SPENDING EVERY WAKING moment consumed by thoughts of nuclear war had finally gotten to Theurer. Day in and day out this horrifying nightmare began to take hold and he found it evolving from a bad dream into something much more dire. As development on *Missile Command* continued, these nightmares began to occur much more frequently, escalating brutally as they grew more vivid and realistic with each passing occurrence. They may have started with a simple explosion, but quickly grew to much more horrifying visions.

For most, something of this nature would be extremely concerning—and it was for Theurer as well, but not enough for him to say anything to anyone about it. Despite working with him on the project every day, he never said a word to Rich Adam. He kept it bottled up, dedicating even more time to finishing the game, hoping these visions would subside once he was able to detach himself after the game's release. He figured that if he couldn't sleep, he might as well be working on the game, and started pulling all-nighters at the office, believing it was a better use of his time than attempting to sleep, only to wake up sweating and in a state of shock. He worked for days on end, often pulling multiple ninety-six-hour shifts.

As his sleep decreased and his obsession increased, these nightmares began to bleed into reality. Theurer lived near Moffett Field, in Santa Clara County, and would often be startled by planes flying overhead, convinced the engine rumble was the sound of an atomic blast heading his way.

After just six months of working on *Missile Command*,

Theurer had done exactly what he was hoping the player would do: he had internalized the game's message, but to a dangerous and unintended extreme. With this sobering realization, he knew that he had finally done it. It worked, though perhaps just a little too well.

Though his internalization was unintended, he knew that this meant he was on to something. He had taken it to the extreme because of his obsession with the project, but he wasn't the only one who was constantly thinking about nuclear war; everyone else was, too. He knew he finally had a real opportunity to share this message with a world that needed to hear it, even if it came at the cost of his sanity.

For Theurer, it was all worth it—even the stress that caused his nightmares. But others disagree, including Barry Krakow, a leading sleep disorder specialist. In the early days of development, Theurer didn't know how to separate the game from the rest of his life. As with anything, putting that much time and effort into any project allows it to seep into unintended aspects of one's life. "[Anything] attended to with great intensity during the day frequently appears in our dreams," explains Krakow, drawing the connection between Theurer's obsession and the way that our brains process sleep. Most of the time, Krakow explains, this isn't really noticeable. We might spend the day with friends doing a single activity for the majority of the day, but it doesn't consume our dreams. But when paired with overwhelming stress and anxiety, there's a pretty good chance that what you spend your time on during the day will make its way into your dreams at night.

It's something we don't really notice most of the time. What we spend our time on seems normal to us, so it doesn't trigger anything unique when we encounter it in our dreams. But nuclear war? Yeah, that's something you remember.

Theurer's reoccurring dreams were terrifying; they weren't

your average nightmares. They felt real, often leaving him questioning whether he was still in this dream state when he woke up. But upon forcing himself to encounter these atrocities constantly, day in and day out, for six months at a time, he began to wear down. The constant overconsumption of such dark and powerful material began to take hold, taking something that was once a terrifying, irregular occurrence and turning it into the new norm.

As development continued, Theurer knew that these nightmares were beginning to become an issue. He had to finish *Missile Command*—and quickly. They had only been working on the game for six months, but it had begun consuming his every thought, something that increasingly worried Theurer as he raced toward the finish line, repeating, "It'll be worth it. It'll be worth it. It'll be . . ."

The Tests Begin

10

F ROM RECRUITMENT TOOLS TO FLASHING MIND CONTROL PAT-
terns, conspiracy theories surrounding arcades and their
most popular titles were rampant during the late 1970s,
often involving mysterious suited figures watching from afar in
arcades.

The public was in a state of distrust. Though events weren't
as dramatic as you might see on television, the Cold War served
as a reminder that life wasn't always as simple as it seemed.
Could you trust those around you? Probably. But what if you
couldn't?

The scenario goes like this: You're at your local arcade one
day and suddenly there's a new game, one you've never seen before. You give it a shot—and immediately die. It's much harder
than the other games in the arcade, but you aren't yet sure if
that's by design or the result of poor programming. Could this
be a purposefully difficult game that's going to become the next
big challenge between you and your friends, or is it just some
poorly designed, unknown arcade game the owner added to
bump up his intake of your hard-earned quarters? Who knows,
but you're hooked.

Your mom has sent you there for a few hours and you have
to make your quarters last the whole time. You're in it to win

it; quarter after quarter, it's all starting to come together—you're figuring out the patterns and adapting, making it farther with each attempt until it finally happens: you make it to the kill screen, the point at which the game can no longer be played, as the player has exceeded the programming capabilities of the hardware.

The screen flashes an incoherent pattern—brainwashing you with a complete mind dump of classified government material before shutting down. You pull your attention back to the room and hear "Mr. Rubens, we need to speak with you," at which point you're inducted into the CIA on the spot.

This is an extreme example, but this is what kids were thinking of at the time—it seemed like something that could be possible, mainly because your friend's cousin in Cleveland heard it had happened, and they never heard from that kid again. We knew your friend's cousin was making it up, but it didn't really matter; there was some part of us that wanted to believe it.

Maybe you didn't even need to reach the kill screen, but instead one day you'd come back to the arcade and the machine would be gone with the arcade owner having "no recollection of that machine." Soon enough, you get a visit where guys in suits are asking if you're "ASS" from the top of the leaderboard, ready to recruit you for a top-secret program.

So you might be thinking, "Um, that sounds like the plot of the 1984 film *The Last Starfighter*." And you'd be right.

People like to believe in such conspiracies. It's the same feeling many share about aliens: you aren't going to be the guy running around telling everyone that you believe aliens are real, but you aren't ruling it out either. That's more or less how the conversation went around these theories.

"Well, they have to recruit from somewhere, don't they?"

"It makes sense as they'd probably want someone who's good with technology!"

"They need young recruits with fast reflexes to train into supersoldiers!"

But was any of it true? Who knows. Perhaps some of it was, but it was likely much stealthier than a group of guys nervously watching from the corner of the arcade. In fact, that group some kid probably saw and told everyone was the government? That was more likely programmers like Dave Theurer and his team running a "field test"—a series of tests where companies like Atari would pay an arcade owner to place their machine inside the arcade for a few days so they could observe player behavior and then make changes where necessary. This was a required step of production at Atari and is still something done with video games today. Nowadays they just bring a focus group of players into a development studio for a day and make them sign a boatload of nondisclosure agreements, but the idea is still the same.

These field tests were vital to the success of the game; not just for squashing bugs and ensuring that what they were asking players to do was feasible, but also to ensure that players were actually having a good time and that they weren't just being distracted by a new shiny cabinet that was a nice break from their usual favorite. Programmers were required to do a few of them for each game, making changes as quickly as possible and burning a new circuit board (or ROM), to get it right back out there for another test. Because of this speed and the importance put on these tests, this was often one of the most stressful times of production—a fact that only amplified the nightmares that Theurer was experiencing.

In order for these tests to take place, he had to have a playable build of the game ready in time to be burned to a ROM and placed in a machine. It wasn't like it is now, where you can just patch in fixes; it had to be ready for the public once it went in that machine.

These tests were a great opportunity for bar or arcade owners. Typically with a normal arcade cabinet, quarters would be split between the venue owner and the cabinet operator. With these field tests, however, Atari would pass 100 percent of the revenue through to owners in exchange for letting the company conduct its tests. All the owners had to do was have one of their staff members keep a tally of how many people were playing on the machine for a specific period of time.

The real challenge came from the secrecy required for this task, as the company had to keep a low profile so word didn't get out it was testing something unreleased. If it did, competitors would show up almost immediately, posing as normal patrons; they'd pull out a small notepad and begun to take note of everything they possibly could about the machine. They'd dump quarter after quarter into it, trying to figure out the gameplay mechanics, systems, and programming tricks so they could create a clone and distribute it prior to the full release of the game being tested.

This is where Atari itself was causing a bit of a slowdown. With just a single programmer assigned to design and create each game, a competing team could easily implement the programming aspects of the design and create a knockoff in a much faster time frame since they didn't need to go through all of the processes that Atari required at the time. They didn't need to field test. They didn't need to go through layers of approval. They'd just find a game that was already designed, take as many notes as they could about it, and immediately attempt to re-create it for immediate release, often beating the original game to market, though with a much inferior product.

Even with that risk ever present, these field tests were vital to figuring out what players thought would be fun. The development team would sit nearby, blending in as typical bar or arcade patrons, and take notes of how players were reacting to the game so they could make changes to the gameplay between field tests and fine-tune aspects of how the game worked.

These tests weren't just for the gameplay, though; they were also used to test how people reacted to the cabinet and their attraction to it. This proved to be an extremely vital aspect of the *Missile Command* tests, as major revisions were made to the cabinet throughout these tests.

Though these tests were stressful, their outcomes reinforced why leadership was so adamant about these tests being such an important part of the overall development process at Atari.

Time lines were different back then though. Developers couldn't spend years working on a game; they had to get it out and get started on the next one. Because of this, Theurer didn't have forever to fix stuff after a field test. Instead, he had to make what changes he wanted to make and get the next one set up. This resulted in an overwhelming schedule for Atari programmers, especially Theurer, who was so focused on getting ready for the next field test that he wouldn't sleep for days on end. In one instance, this caught up with him, as he didn't leave the office for nearly four days—ninety-six hours straight—as his deadline was quickly approaching, and he wouldn't have been able to finish in time working mere eight-hour days.

It got to the point where, though he had finished the work he needed to on the game, he lost motor functions and was unable to operate the machine that burned the ROMs for the arcade cabinets. He had finished what they needed for the next round of field tests, but physically couldn't manufacture it to take with them the next day. "I couldn't remember how to punch the buttons on the keyboard," says Theurer. He had finished all he needed to, but he had fried his brain in the process and just couldn't figure out how to work a keyboard anymore.

Unable to continue on his own, Theurer ignored the signs that his body was telling him to take a break; ignoring the metaphysical alarm bells ringing in his ear, he opted to call in a favor.

He called a friend to come to the office and work the machine for him. He explained to his friend what they needed do and exactly how to do it. *Missile Command* was ready for the field test that next day, but Theurer was left exhausted and barely functioning.

These were the lengths to which Theurer's obsession grew. His constant striving for perfection left him working his body to the point of physical deprivation. Hearing stories like this, it becomes a lot easier to understand the obsessive nature behind the project for Theurer and see how easy it can be for a single thought to completely take over one's every waking moment. It's no wonder that his mind had room for these visions to manifest themselves into obsessive nightmares that, even once his sleep habits recovered, couldn't be completely flushed from his subconscious.

Theurer isn't alone in this type of all-encompassing obsession; it's something many creative people struggle with, and it can be found in video game creation backstories to this day. Following the indie gaming revolution of 2008-2011, there were hundreds—if not thousands—of creators out there who believed that they alone could build something to be enjoyed by millions of people. These developers didn't have a ton of experience or a specific story to tell, so often their game's narratives centered around their own personal stories. This personal drive to tell a story is different from what Theurer experienced, but the end result is still the same.

While Theurer and others at Atari might have been responsible for some of the confusion around these field tests and the urban legends that surrounded them, there are plenty of such stories they had nothing to do with. In a time when espionage was rampant and homegrown spies were one of the commonly held fears of the everyday American, it wasn't totally unusual for people to see what they wanted to see.

Atari employees sneaking over to a machine to insert a new test ROM into the game could easily be mistaken for government officials pulling data from the machine to start recruitment, or spies dropping information that could hurt the United States. There were rumors flying around about all types of games, not just *Missile Command*, but the game's thematic elements and the anticommunist spirit of the country at the time helped lend some credibility in the eyes of conspirators (or those they were just trying to convince) that cemented theories surrounding this game slightly more than those of other games.

For most, they were nothing more than silly chatter spouted by the same conspiracy theorists who were still shouting that the CIA killed President John F. Kennedy and that the Apollo moon landings were faked, but for some, the fact that it was connected to a relatively new medium that was experiencing nearly supernatural growth added just a tinge of believability. In their eyes, it made total sense that the government would try to recruit those who were able to decode a game's basic systems and find a way to circumvent them, all in the short time frame that a single quarter provided. That kind of high-functioning approach to creative problem solving was exactly the type of thing government agencies were looking for, even—or in some cases, *especially*—at such a young age. When it came to in-game performance, some thought top scorers were sure to be extremely capable of the piloting of aircraft or other combat vehicles— much like the plot of *The Last Starfighter* or *Future Man*. The former held greater weight despite being the more ludicrous of the two, if only because it was the dream of every teenage boy at the time.

Finally, there were rumors of secret machines placed in arcades that were programmed to deliver mind-controlling information via the flashes of light on the screen. While there's no definitive proof that any such cabinets ever existed, that doesn't stop people from claiming they experienced it at the time. One such rumor that is often cited is that of *Polybius*, a mysterious arcade cabinet that is reported to have appeared in Portland, Oregon, arcades in 1981. These reports claim that those who played it ended up suffering from amnesia, night terrors, and a host of other ailments, and that men in black suits were sneaking into the arcades later to retrieve data from the machines.

Then, one day, all the machines disappeared without a trace. They were never seen again until 1998, when a post online appeared from someone who claimed to be in possession of a *Polybius* logic board. Many consider this post to be the real start of *Polybius*, with revisionist history building on unsubstantiated conspiracies theories to fill in the backstory. With these conspiracy theories flying around at the time, it's likely that people just piggybacked off the popular theory to help attach some validity to their claims, but whether it actually existed or not, it's another example of just how profoundly the culture of mistrust and misdirection spread roots in everything, including pop culture.

Regardless, Theurer refutes all claims of outside influence on *Missile Command*, as does the rest of his former team at Atari. Just like most other arcade urban legends, these are patently false. Though it's fun to imagine that something much bigger was going on, anyone who did see anything was likely a part of one of Atari's many field tests and was lucky enough to take part in it.

The endless urban legends from this period are prime examples of just how deeply video games had engulfed the American consciousness. Even when they weren't playing, people wanted these games to be a part of their life. They wanted there to be a bigger story, something that went far beyond what they knew to be true at the time. It was like a ghost story: it didn't matter if you really believed it or not; there was always that 1 percent that thought maybe it was true, so you might as well pass it along to your friends.

A kill screen is an endgame state of an arcade release. Essentially, it's the point where the game can no longer progress any further, and it was required to stop the game due to technical limitations. *Missile Command* does have a kill screen of sorts, but it doesn't work in the same way. For *Missile Command*, the game reaches a state in which you just continue to play forever, doing the same thing over and over again with new cities being awarded with each round under the game's Marathon Settings. It was extremely common for arcade games to encounter a kill screen at some point and, in many famous examples, like *Pac-Man*, was actually the result of a design flaw. Many of these games weren't programmed with an official ending in mind. For the most part, you just played for as long as you could, and the game ended when you lost all your lives. There wasn't a final boss, final level, nothing. This meant that if players were good enough, they could continue to increase their score or reach a numerical point where the game's processor couldn't handle it anymore and crashed. It's essentially what everyone feared would happen with computers when Y2K came at the turn of the twenty-first century: the games weren't made to accommodate numbers that high, and would crash once they rolled over to a certain point. For *Pac-Man*, this manifested in the form of a perfect score that cannot be beat. This disappeared when we reached the 16-bit era, as hardware improved and programmers no longer had issues with the score exceeding the limited amount of memory available.

Into the Wild

11

I N MODERN GAMING AND COMPUTER SCIENCE GENERALLY, THE term "beta" is thrown around pretty loosely. It used to be that beta tests would go live six months or so before a video game was set to hit the shelves so that its developers could actually implement any changes that needed to be made. Now, more often than not, very few drastic changes based on player feedback will actually go into effect, and a beta test is seen as a marketing opportunity to get the game into players' hands prior to release. Back in the day, though, these field tests were a massive part of the development process.

When Dave Theurer, Rich Adam, and their team at Atari did field tests for *Missile Command*, they were making substantial changes after each visit. Theurer's style has always been to run through as many options as possible to find out what plays the best, so these field tests were heaven to him—that is, if you don't count the accompanying stress. Being able to get real-time feedback on what players did or didn't like before sending that information out as changes to be pressed onto millions of arcade boards was extremely valuable.

How did players like the trackball? How did they like the colors? Was the game too difficult? Was it fun? These were all questions that field tests sought to answer. As Theurer got his answers, he continued work on the project, pouring in more hours than ever before as he neared the finish line. He knew he was getting close and that he couldn't take much more of the hell that the game was putting him through. Sure, he could have quit, but that wasn't who Theurer was. He wanted to get his message out there, and knew that it could only succeed if he did it right then.

With deadlines in place and workers at the ready, they needed to start finalizing designs to get *Missile Command* out the door on time. One major aspect of this was the cabinet that would house the game. As with most games at the time, the cabinet was a player's first impression. If you didn't have a cool cabinet, the chances of someone giving your game a shot were less than optimal. During the arcade craze of the late 1970s and early 1980s, you really needed to stand out—and that meant more than having pretty artwork.

As a result, Theurer and Adam decided to do something totally different with the cabinet, something that hadn't been done before. They wanted to replace the typical marquee top of an arcade cabinet with a function light panel that was tied to events in the game. This attempt to bring the game to the physical world was something entirely unique, and they weren't sure how players were going to react.

The panel would display status indicators about your cities and how close incoming missiles were to destroying them. It was extremely cool, and no other arcade game at the time had it. Yet upon taking it out into the wild for some field tests, they realized a fatal flaw of their unique design: players had to take their eyes off the gameplay. As they progressed in the game, they kept looking up at the panel, which made Theurer and Adam happy, but when they looked back at the screen they had lost track of what they were doing. At high-level play, this loss of focus was undesirable.

It sounds so obvious in retrospect that this wouldn't work, but they were so focused on making the cabinet design cool that they hadn't really thought about how it would play out on a practical level. As a result of this discovery, they decided to remove the light-filled panel and create a very simple design that would catch the eye of potential players but leave the gameplay to do the talking. "[The players] kept looking up to check the status lights and stuff, so we just chopped off the whole top of the cabinet," recalls Theurer, who has the prototype in his garage to this day.

There was another hidden benefit of getting rid of this panel: cost reduction. At the time, having to manufacture an arcade cabinet for every copy of the game was a massive cost. In fact, even without the light panel, *Missile Command*'s build cost, not including labor, was $871. "[We] saved ourselves a whole lot of money without hurting the gameplay any," Theurer remembers.

With this reduction in scope, they were finally ready to wrap up production and send the game off to manufacturing. Theurer and Adam poured countless hours into double-checking every aspect of what they had done. With these small teams, they didn't have massive quality control departments that ensured everything was up to the company's standards. They only had their team. All the same, they pushed through, knowing they were so close to completion.

Deprived of sleep and haunted by his own creation, Theurer finished up his last few tasks, becoming emotional as he pressed the key to start the final compiling of the build for the circuit board they would put into production. It had only been a few months since Theurer had started on *Missile Command*, but it felt like eternity, and the emotional toll was much greater than he had ever imagined it would be when he set out on the project. He had entered as a man determined to finish a project and get his name out there; he left reconsidering whether he ever wanted to make another game again. The cost of getting his message out there was high, but he was elated to finally be done with it.

Theurer finished the build and handed it off to the engineering team to make it a reality. They began work so that it could be sent off to the manufacturing plant down the road to begin pressing the boards. Getting in his car to drive home, Theurer hoped it had all been worth it. He wouldn't know for sure until a few months later, when the game was ready to be sent out to arcades, but for now he was content. Who knows, perhaps he might finally get some rest.

WHEN THE FIRST completed cabinets began shipping out later in 1980, Theurer sat at the office working on his next project, *Tempest*. With everyone at the office fawning over *Missile Command* during tests, he was as confident as he could be that the game was going to be a hit. He eagerly awaited results back from arcades and couldn't help but be excited to know that the first players were experiencing what he had dedicated his life so fully to for the last few months. It had been a passion of his and he wanted so badly for that to show in the message he crafted into the gameplay.

As the game hit arcades and players were given the first opportunities to play it, the feedback started rolling in. They loved it; it was an instant hit. It was hailed for its uniqueness, color graphics, and challenging score-based gameplay, all of which were massive draws for arcade games at the time. It was truly revolutionary, like nothing most people had seen before, and arcade fans actually traveled to be among the first to play it at one of the arcades that received the first few units. Most of all, it was extremely fun even in spite of the moral limitations he had imposed on the game.

Theurer was ecstatic. They had done it: they had taken an idea pulled from a magazine advertisement seen in passing and turned it into the most popular arcade game in the world. It wasn't an easy task, and it certainly wasn't without its casualties along the way, but looking back on it, their work pushed the boundary of what was possible in an arcade game at a time when most people were just trying to produce as many as possible. They had done something different, and the overwhelming response reflected that creativity.

It was the most popular game in arcades at the time, a title that most game developers would be proud to hold; even so, for Theurer it was always about the underlying message about the state of the world at the time. He wanted to craft an experience that lasted beyond a quarter, that pushed players to experience the fragility of war through their own eyes. And that's exactly what he did, even if most players didn't realize it at the time. Just as Theurer had been affected by the message of the game, so had his players. Many of them were getting their first taste of what nuclear war might actually look like. They had heard about it everywhere they went, unable to escape the conflicting narratives surrounding its simultaneous narratives of destruction and protection, but now they were actually witnessing a version of it.

Rhetoric was strong at the time. The general underlying theme of all discussions around nuclear war was that the United States would never strike first. It wasn't about engaging in war, it was about protecting ourselves from war. "We aren't going to do anything, but if they do and we're going down, they're going down with us." This concept of mutually assured destruction left many confused about the right path forward.

But Theurer's message was different. What if we *didn't* do this? If we weren't going to survive an attack, what good would it do us to counterattack? What if we instead focused on addressing this devastating scenario from the start and came up with a better solution than stockpiling weapons that wouldn't benefit us? These were the questions he wanted people to ask. He wanted to give people a look at how nuclear war would end in the hope that they would realize just how devastating it could be. He wanted them to know that there is no winner in nuclear war.

Most people didn't get any of this from the game. They had fun and they kept coming back, watching as their cities blew up and moving on with their day as if nothing had happened, but it had lasting no effect on them. And that was okay. Theurer knew he wasn't going to get his message across to everybody. Heck, he knew only a small percentage of people might even be able to detach the scenario from the game to really think through it, and even then, they might disagree with the basic premise. He didn't care; even getting the message across to one person was worth it.

It took time for this message to truly take hold; it wasn't something that people were able to grab hold of immediately. They didn't have time to extract deep commentary about the Cold War because they were still too close to it; they were living in it. The message was there, and people were digesting it, but it wasn't yet clear how much of an impact it could have on the average player's understanding of the situation. It was a connection that most were unable to make at the time, but the hope was for long-term impact.

Theurer knew that this would be the case. That's why he needed something that wasn't just fun, but was so fun and unique that it would be capable of lasting for generations to come; that's what he needed from *Missile Command*. And while the game's qualities and technical achievements cannot be understated, it was this mind-set and Theurer's approach to the message that allowed it to achieve the success that it did. Without that, *Missile Command* would have been just another arcade game. It needed that lens to captivate the audience, and captivate it did. It was fun, exciting, and joyous to play. It captured the American consciousness and took hold of an industry in a way that few games had done before. To this day, we're still in awe of *Missile Command* as a technical and entertainment marvel, despite the fact that it was surpassed technologically in the years following its release. We were given something so basic as an arcade defender game, but with a complicated and deep message that even today works to show that games can be more than just entertainment; they can be art.

The Public Loves It

12

I N THE YEARS FOLLOWING ITS RELEASE, *MISSILE COMMAND* remained a steady icon of both arcade gaming and 1980s culture. It had elevated video gaming content and goals far beyond what was standard, choosing instead to craft an important narrative around the gameplay itself. Most games have a narrative, but very few craft an external narrative that isn't just a setup for the gameplay but is instead a result of that gameplay. *Missile Command* stood out from the crowd because of this. It wasn't just an arcade game from the 1980s; it was *the* arcade game from the 1980s.

The game became a staple of any popular arcade and went on to become one of Atari's most popular machines at the time. It was a hot seller, and that success translated well to its developers, Dave Theurer and Rich Adam. Not only had they broken the first-game curse at Atari (a feat that would later be renamed Theurer's Law, as he was the first to actually accomplish it), but he'd also created the hottest game on the market. Atari couldn't keep up with demand, spinning up its local production facility to produce more cabinets than could ever have been imagined. In the end, Atari ended up producing more than twenty thousand arcade cabinets, which was a massive success for both Atari and Theurer. While this was certainly no *Space Invaders* or *Asteroids*, which went on to sell 360,000 units and 100,000 units, respectively, *Missile Command* was extremely successful, securing a spot as one of the twenty most-sold arcade games of all time, according to IGN.

Theurer and Adam were propelled from first-time project leads to superstars at Atari. They had taken something basic and turned it into a masterpiece. This now allowed them to do whatever they wanted. They could take another project from Steve Calfee or they could come up with something on their own. While they were figuring out what they would do now that the project was done, the game was continuing to see massive success across the world and communities began forming around their love for the game.

With such a large aspect of arcade communities being focused on score-based competition, *Missile Command* was a perfect fit. They had followed Atari founder Nolan Bushnell's rule of "easy to learn, difficult to master" precisely and, as a result, created a game that could essentially run forever without worrying about someone beating the game—meaning they could compete via score battles for as long as they could go. And compete they did.

In late 1980, when the game released, we were halfway through the appointed "golden era of arcade gaming" and competition was all the rage. It wasn't uncommon to be playing with friends and drop everything you were doing when you got word that someone was attempting to break a record at your local arcade. Arcades were the place to be, so seeing someone do something special in your spot was a big event, especially for kids who found the arcade to be their primary hangout spot. As these communities formed, it became clear that this dedicated audience would grab *Missile Command* and never let go. The game was perfect for competitive play: it was endless (more or less), extremely complex, and based entirely on score. You didn't have to keep all your cities alive if you didn't want to; as long as you had one left, you were still in the game. *Missile Command*'s unique approach to gameplay meant that you could go about it a million different ways, and new techniques were popping up all the time.

You may have heard of Billy Mitchell, the loud, bombastic, mullet-rocking world record holder whom many love to hate. Mitchell, along with others, were some of the world's first pro gamers, long before you could become one while still in high school and make a career out of it. It was less about twitch re- actions and more about being able to understand the patterns behind the gameplay and capitalize on them, but it was just as difficult as ever.

At the time that *Missile Command* was released, these guys were looked upon as rock stars. If Billy Mitchell was going to make an appearance at your local arcade, it felt like the whole town came out for it. He'd pick a machine and start trying to break the high score on it as dozens of arcade goers looked on in disbelief. Despite the game's popularity at the time, the *Missile Command* scene never really had any rock stars. Sure, there were a few guys who held records and were looked up to by big *Missile Command* fans, but there was no one king at the top of the mountain . . . at least, not yet.

This changed in 1981 as one of these competitive players stumbled on *Missile Command* for the first time. Little did he know it would become his obsession as he engaged in a lifelong battle for supremacy. Before we get too deep into this, know that despite how crazy this sounds, it's entirely true, even if some participants don't want you to know that. Now strap in and prepare yourself for some betrayal and intrigue. It doesn't get better than this.

London, 1981

Enter Tony Temple. An ordinary man by all accounts, Temple wasn't like the rest of the competitive gaming community. He didn't spend years in an arcade making a name for himself as he took over the arcade's top spot on each game; he just stumbled into it. One day Temple was walking home and saw the *Missile Command* cabinet through the window of an arcade. It was striking, unlike anything he had ever seen before, and he couldn't resist the urge to give it a shot. The game had just arrived from the United States, and though it had taken nearly a year for it to make the trek across the ocean, somehow no one really knew it was coming and he was able to start sinking his coins into it before almost anyone else.

He was fascinated by the trackball—he'd never seen anything like it, and fell in love with it. Most games used simple joysticks at the time, so the trackball intimidated traditional arcade goers, but not Temple. He put in his coin and began to play, experiencing total sensory overload as he defended his cities from incoming attacks. It was frantic and powerful, instilling an immediate sense of fear in him.

Even in the UK, being relatively removed from the front lines of the Cold War, the tension coursed through his veins, adding to the fear he experienced through the unique setup of the game's controls.

Temple returned day after day, putting more and more time into the game. Eventually he became quite good at it, as he was able to capitalize on this frantic nature and use it to his advantage. The very aspect that drew him to *Missile Command* drove others away, allowing him to become fully immersed and continue building his skills without needing to hop off the cabinet for anyone else in line. He enjoyed the challenge, but others didn't. "It handed you your ass every single time," Temple remembers affectionately.

He didn't play anything else, only *Missile Command*. Because of his rabid dedication, he quickly became known around the arcade as the Missile Command Guy, a title he quite enjoyed. Admittedly, he was a one-trick pony, but that was by choice. At the time there wasn't much competition around him for *Missile Command*, as evidenced by the fact that he earned that nickname. This gave him the opportunity to compete against himself and to continue to hone his skills. He started worrying less about other players and focused on increasing his score, seeing how high he could push it, with no limit in sight. Then it happened: he hit a new high score, and found that the limit did exist . . . even if it wasn't supposed to.

Score: 810,000

The first time Tony Temple hit 810,000 points, he was in his local London arcade, just as he was most days. Without much competition, and with a fan base beginning to build at his local arcade, Temple often drew a small crowd, including the arcade's owner, who came to watch him performing at such a high level. Temple was able to hit 810,000 and, upon doing so, bonus cities started to appear out of nowhere, sending everyone into a panic, including Temple. Assuming the machine was broken and in danger of destroying itself, the owner ran over to it and pulled the power cord from the wall. "God bless him," remembers Temple. "He honestly thought the thing was going to catch fire." They didn't know what to do—no one had ever gotten this far before.

At the time, most video games had multiple settings that could be engaged in case you wanted to have different modes enabled. *Missile Command* had a few, though it was typically set to Marathon Settings, as that was the most common and recommended mode for arcade play. Yet Temple discovered that under these settings you could receive a bonus city every 10,000 points once you hit 810,000. If you were able to do this, the game was essentially over as far as Temple was concerned. Handing out bonus cities at that frequency meant that you would eventually gain cities faster than you could lose them, turning it more into a game of endurance than skill. It took away the challenge for him—he had reached the peak. Luckily the bar was set high, and scoring 810,000 wasn't a regular occurrence for him, but as competition continued to dwindle, he began to fear the worst. Things may have been fierce in the United States, but there wasn't anything happening in the United Kingdom. Eventually there was no one left to beat, not even himself. He'd reached 810,000, and there wasn't anyone else competing around him. He was too skilled for his own good. He never saw competition in 1982; it was too late, as interest in a competitive scene had mostly waned in his area.

Soon enough the cabinets began to disappear from arcades—often converted to house other games, smashed, or just dumped in the trash, to be replaced by newer, more updated games. It was the middle of the golden era of arcade gaming, but none of these other games grabbed Temple like *Missile Command* had. One day he walked into his local arcade and realized he had played his last game: the machine had disappeared, and so had Temple's dreams of competing.

The Revival

As time passed, *Missile Command* was released outside of arcades, but it just wasn't the same for Temple. "I remember playing on a PC and thinking, 'This just isn't as good as the arcade experience,'" he recalls. If it wasn't as good as the arcade, he wasn't going to play it. With each subsequent release, Temple hoped he would find a glimmer of the perfection he had experienced all those years ago, but it was lost. PlayStation, PlayStation 2, PC—nothing did it for him. He needed the unique controls to match the gameplay. It just wasn't *Missile Command* to him without them. So he moved on.

The years continued to fly by. Then, when Temple was in his late thirties, he randomly bumped into someone who collected old arcade machines. They began talking, yammering on about the good old days, and Temple brought up his fondness for *Missile Command* all those years before. The man stopped mid-conversation and said, "Oh, come with me."

Temple followed the man back to his house, and deep in his basement, there it was, right in front of him, as if perfectly and meticulously removed from the farthest corners of his nostalgia-ridden memories: a *Missile Command* arcade cabinet. At first unable to speak due to shock, he finally muttered, "My God . . ."

Flooded with emotions and vivid memories of his best days, he couldn't help but relive them: the frantic play, the celebration, the elation when reaching a new personal milestone. He recalled the accomplishment he felt when he found a new pattern in the machine and was able to tame it to his advantage. This run-in was the final push he needed to regain the sense of competition and passion he had been chasing for so many years. "I had to have one," he recalls. "I've just got to have that machine."

And off the two went, finding a machine for Temple. This was quite the task, as most of the *Missile Command* machines that were available in the UK had, at one point or another, been destroyed or repurposed when the arcade owners no longer had a use for them. Finding one wouldn't be an easy process, but they were determined. They asked around, talking to collectors and former arcade owners, eventually stumbling on one—or what was left of one—for sale. It was pretty beat up, not at all in the same pristine shape as the one in the man's basement, but it was Tony's. Even a busted machine was worth the world to him. He was determined enough that he had no issue with the work required to fix it. Lucky for him, that's exactly what his new friend had just done. Over the course of the next few months, they went to work restoring the once-junked cabinet to its former glory. It took an exceptional amount of work and would never have been possible without the help of his new friend, but they did it, and the machine now resides in Temple's basement, bringing some of the grandeur that his local arcade once exuded. Now that he had the cabinet, he was ready to get playing. What came next formed the basis for everything *Missile Command* has come to represent for Temple.

The Discovery

Though his early formative years with *Missile Command* were the guiding light for his desire to own the game himself, Tony Temple's skill and passion in his second life with *Missile Command* would find a spotlight at heights never before achieved, and decades after his first encounter with the game.

Following the completion of his restoration, he finally sat down to play his first game *on his own cabinet*. It was finally happening, and Temple couldn't contain his excitement. He had done all that work purely for nostalgia reasons, but once he played that first game, he realized something. "I've still got the old chops," he said to himself, "my skills are still there."

He began digging around on the internet for other *Missile Command* players to see if the game had any kind of competitive community. He hadn't been able to do this the first time around—the internet wasn't around then, and he had to rely on those in his local arcade for information. He found the high scores that were widely considered to be the best at the time and was a bit surprised. "Well, I reckon I can get those," he said to himself. He'd excelled in his earlier years, and it didn't seem like his skills had deteriorated that much. He figured it was worth a shot. Looking at the scores again, he realized there was something different from when he had played the first time. These scores were all achieved on Tournament Settings, something Temple had never heard of before. He wasn't even aware there were multiple settings for the game; he just thought everyone had the same game and had encountered the same issues he had. Once he did some digging, he realized just how big of a game changer this was for him.

He quickly discovered that he had been playing on Marathon Settings all along, as had most people who casually enjoyed *Missile Command*. But Marathon Settings suffered from the 810,000-point bug Temple had encountered all these years ago. Because of this bug, most people didn't consider it to be a truly competitive mode. They wanted something that was a challenge without giving the player handouts to survive. This is where Tournament Settings come in. In this mode, you get your six cities to start and that's it. There are no bonus cities for achieving certain milestones or progression points; once you lose your cities, they're gone forever. As you might have guessed, this appealed to Temple, and he was hooked once again.

Had he known all along that this mode existed and there was still a competitive community formed around the game, things wouldn't have ended so limply back in 1982. He was rejuvenated and excited about the prospect of competing again. With a newfound understanding of modern competitive *Missile Command*, Temple went to his basement and opened up his cabinet. He dug out the manual and started tinkering around to enable Tournament Settings. If he was going to play competitively again, he was going to do it right.

Though Temple didn't find Marathon Settings to be challenging, many others did, and competition continued to flourish. At the same time that Temple had initially given up, one man had just finished a thirty-hour game of *Missile Command,* taking place entirely on Marathon Settings. With a score of 41,399,845, Jody Bowles became the new world champion.

This record was short-lived, as his record was doubled the following year by Victor Ali, who was reported to play for fifty-six hours straight to achieve this score. This record stood for more than thirty years, until 2013, when Victor Sandberg surpassed Ali's score by 1,431,040 points. Sandberg later broke his own record with a score of 103,809,990, a feat that took nearly seventy-two hours to accomplish.

Judging by the numbers, Temple's assumption that it was all an endurance game was correct. In order to compete you had to be willing to play for days at a time. As you played, you built up a reserve of extra cities that many players would use to give themselves breaks away from the game. You couldn't build up too many, though—if it went above 256 cities, the game would crash, making the challenge much more difficult, as you had to keep track of that over time.

As of 2018, there is still much competition for the title of world champion.

Little Time for a New Record: 2005–2006

Temple felt alive. He had not only rebuilt something that was such a large part of his life all those years earlier but also discovered that he wasn't alone in his love for *Missile Command.* Toward the end of his time with the game in the early 1980s, he had started to feel as if he was the only one who cared about *Missile Command* in the UK. Sure, people cared enough to watch him, but his standing as the Missile Command Guy should tell you everything you need to know about how much competition there was. He now hoped that having the internet would mean he didn't have to be alone, even if he was the only one in the UK really competing. For something as physical as arcade gaming, it was surprising to him to see such a strong on-line community built around the game, whether they were playing it or just watching as former players.

He made the switch to Tournament Settings and set off to beat what he believed to be the standing world record at the time. He put in the work, his skills quickly coming back to him, and reached the 1,000,000-point mark with ease, a feat he deemed to be quite significant based on other competition. Despite the large online community built around competitive arcade play, there still weren't a ton of people playing *Missile Command* competitively at the time. Because of this, Temple's score attempts really lit up the scene. Though he may have left the spotlight nearly twenty-five years earlier, Temple was regaining notoriety in the scene and was beginning to gain an audience determined to see him crowned world champion. It was certainly nothing like the arcade rock star days of the 1980s, but he was just happy to know people were out there rooting for him.

In just a short time Temple had surpassed even his original skill level; he was continuously posting scores over 1,000,000 points. Believing he was in the running for the world record, he got in touch with Walter Day, the founder of Twin Galaxies, to get an update on the competitive scene and where his own score landed on the charts. Even to this day, Twin Galaxies is the be-all and end-all of competitive arcade gaming. Anytime you've seen a story about record-setting competitive play, whether in *Donkey Kong* or *Pac-Man*, it went through Walter Day and

Twin Galaxies. Just as Guinness is synonymous with world records, so are Day and Twin Galaxies for arcade gaming records. Day held competitions and flew around the world to help officiate record-setting runs; if it had anything to do with competitive play, he was there in his famous custom Twin Galaxies video-game referee jersey.

> Walter Day was the founder of Twin Galaxies, a video game record-keeping company that is widely regarded as the gold standard for world record scores. The company has found itself at the center of many controversies that all stem from score impropriety over the decades that Twin Galaxies has been in operation. Whether falsified scores or unclear guidelines, there's never been a shortage of something to debate about Twin Galaxies.

If anyone knew anything about the current competitive scene for *Missile Command*, it was going to be Walter Day. Unfortunately for Temple, he didn't have good news. Temple's score was short of the current world record set at around 1,690,000 points. Temple may not have held a high enough score to claim the title, but Day continued to encourage him to compete. He clearly showed promise, and it was just a matter of time before that score gap shrank. For Day, it was even more exciting to know that there were people competing in *Missile Command* again. It was a classic for many, but had been shunted to the side in favor of more modern, technically challenging games. Everything that made *Missile Command* special—the beautifully colorful graphics, the unique control setup, the antinuclear narrative—also made it a product of the time. As newer games made their way into the scene, *Missile*

Command was easier to replace than other classics like *Pac-Man* or *Space Invaders*.

Day was especially happy to see someone building out a competitive scene in the UK. Even if Temple wasn't competing with anyone else in Britain, Day liked the story of it all. Most of Twin Galaxies' records across all titles were tracked in the United States, so he liked the rivalry this added to the scene. With most records being in the US, it felt like an invasion from the outside anytime Temple came close to the mark. He wanted to put the UK—and himself—on the map for competitive play, and he would stop at nothing to accomplish it.

Perhaps the most important challenge of all came at the end of that conversation. "As it happens, we're talking to Guinness," said Walter Day, "If you can beat that world record by the end of March 2006, there's a good chance we can get you into the *Guinness Book of World Records*." That was all Temple needed to hear. He was going to beat that record, and he was going to beat it good. At the time, it was one of the highest accomplishments a competitive arcade gamer could hope for.

It wasn't anything like modern e-sports. There was no stadium filled with adoring fans, no multimillion-dollar prize money, no major glory. In 2005, competition wasn't anywhere near as developed as it is now. You couldn't live on winning tournaments—the prize money barely covered the costs of traveling to the event and competing. No one was making this a full-time job, but that wasn't really the purpose. The purpose was to build a legacy. If you could set a record and create a following, you were among the best. And that's just what Temple intended to do.

In 2005 Temple attended an arcade gaming convention in the UK. For those in attendance, it was a celebration of the games they'd spent their whole lives playing, even if the rest of the gaming community had left those games behind in favor of newer titles. It was a chance to get back into the games they'd once dedicated so many coins to and, in some cases, do so in front of a live audience. As a part of this convention, they had flown in Walter Day and Billy Mitchell, among other arcade competitors, to make appearances and play some competitive games onstage for the audience. As a result, Temple was able to play a game of *Missile Command* in front of a live audience.

He hadn't met these arcade legends before; he'd only seen them online and on the scoreboard. Though he was nervous, he was confident that he could perform when put on the spot. Under all the pressure in the world from performing in front of these legends and a massive audience of fans who had just watched them, Temple scored 1,500,000 points, just shy of the world record. Though everyone was disappointed that he wasn't able to beat the standing record, what he'd just done had been extremely impressive, both to Temple and the audience.

From that point on he was sold. He wanted to compete, and he would stop at nothing short of 1,695,266 on his quest for the title of world champion. It was his sole mission. "I played my guts out," he remembers, putting in time every day to improve. Temple hadn't been playing all that long since rediscovering this passion, but he knew he was already operating at 80 percent capacity. He didn't know everything there was to know, but he knew that improving in a few key areas would help his score drastically, and he was fine with putting in the time to learn these. It was the only way he was going to be able to reliably get a winning score past 1,695,265.

He raced home the second the expo was over and set up his video camera pointed at the screen of his cabinet. He was going to do it, but he'd need it on video if it were to be accepted by Twin Galaxies. He was inspired by what he'd seen at the expo and threw himself into it fully, half expecting it to be a relatively quick feat. Instead, he tried and failed hundreds of times.

It was brutal. Set up the camera, hit record, start the game, fail, walk over to the camera, and restart; repeat one hundred more times that day before finally calling it a night. This went on for months as Temple became more and more aware of the looming March 2006 deadline. He was still confident he could do it, but with every failed attempt, things began to look bleaker.

March was nearing, and Temple knew this was his last shot to make something happen. While he loved the return to competitive *Missile Command*, he needed a win—he needed to show that there was something bigger for him here. He needed to beat the record. He knew that if he could do it, he could cement his status in the competitive community, despite his location. If he wasn't able to, there was no telling when his next shot might be.

He tried and tried; starting the tape, stopping the tape, time and time again. It was a tiresome process, but he wanted every detail of his record-breaking run captured, both for Walter Day at Twin Galaxies and also for himself. Though the competition was fierce and he faced extreme difficulties in breaking this record, Temple just loved *Missile Command* and never wanted to let that enjoyment escape in the process.

With just days left before the deadline, Temple knew he had to throw himself into this completely. With everything that *Missile Command* meant to him, he'd be kicking himself if he let this opportunity to be immortalized alongside his favorite game pass him by. He would put in the hours, running back-to-back-to-back attempts until he finally did it—*if* he finally did it.

Then, on March 9, 2006, he had the game of his life. He pulled together everything he had in him, all the passion and skills, a lifetime of love for the game, and beat the 1,695,265-point record that had stood since 1985. In fact, he didn't just beat it, he destroyed it, setting a mark never believed to be possible in competitive *Missile Command*: 1,967,830. He was ecstatic. With blood rushing through his veins, he ran to the camera and stopped the recording, ensuring everything was just as it needed to be for his submission. It was as if the pressure had finally built to a point that his body found the skills that had been hidden deep within him for so long. He celebrated, realizing the gravity of what he had just accomplished: he was now the world's best *Missile Command* player.

In his excitement he almost forgot the most critical next step: he needed to send the tape to be verified by Robert Mruczek, head referee at Twin Galaxies, to be included in the *Guinness Book of World Records*. He made a backup copy of the tape, ensuring nothing would get in the way of him and his title, and sent it off to New York. Though this was the culmination of years of play for Temple, it was just the start. This is where the fun begins.

To the Mecca: 2008

With his new title of world champion on full display for the world to see, Temple felt as though he had finally conquered the beast. He wasn't done playing though—not by a long shot. Instead he played more than ever before, enjoying it just as much as he had back in 1981. For Temple, it was never really about just beating the record; he wanted to create a legacy that went far beyond one score. He wanted his skills to be so well known that they transcended the game itself. He wanted to show he was the best to ever play the game constantly, not just that one time he got a high score. He wanted to continually push himself and the score higher and higher, showing that he was the greatest of all time (the GOAT, as most refer to it)— and he wanted to have some fun in the process.

For arcade players, Funspot Family Entertainment Center at Weirs Beach is a heaven of sorts. Located in the small town of Laconia, New Hampshire, home to only 16,470 people, Funspot is the mecca for arcade gaming, sporting the title of the world's largest arcade, with what some believe to be the largest collection of *Missile Command*–era arcade games. Because of the wide selection of games available and the legacy associated with the venue, it's widely regarded as the best possible arcade at which to set a world record and in 2008, this came to a head as Funspot played host to the Tenth Annual International Classic Video Game and Pinball Tournament. This was a massive event—one of the largest ever in the arcade gaming community—and it attracted the best players from around the world to one venue for multiple days of competition.

Temple had made it a habit to take an annual trip out to Funspot to soak up the culture and meet other players, but this was an event he couldn't miss. He booked a plane ticket and made the trek across the Atlantic to New Hampshire. Little did he know this trip would be unlike any other.

The second Temple entered Funspot, people recognized him. They'd seen him online and knew what he was there for. With his infectious personality, bald head, and British accent, he stood out a bit, too, so it was easy for people to figure out who he was right away. As he walked around and took in the spectacle of the event, people started to follow, hoping they'd get the chance to see him play *Missile Command*. He was the world champion, after all. He wasn't there to compete; he just wanted to have a great time, but he couldn't help himself from playing a few games.

He found the *Missile Command* machine and pulled up a stool, sitting down for a casual game to pass the time. What came next was nothing short of magical. From the second he put the quarter in the machine, everyone there could tell it was going to be something special. Casually, as if no one was there watching him, Temple just started to play. He quickly shot up past 1,000,000 points, and the crowd went wild, but then they realized what was happening. He passed 1,500,000. He passed 1,690,000—the previous record before him. Then they realized just what they might be seeing: a new world record run. As Temple approached the 1,900,000 mark, the intensity grew. For Temple, it had started as just another game, but for the crowd, it was a euphoric experience as they watched what was clearly some of the best *Missile Command* play ever seen unfolding in front of their eyes. He got closer and closer to his previous record when, suddenly, he passed it and celebrated as the crowd went wild. They were seeing history in the making—and it wasn't on the stage. He hadn't even been attempting to set the record, but there he was, just being Tony Temple.

When he finally lost his last city, he wrapped up with a final score of 2,200,000, setting a new world record and becoming the first person to break the 2,000,000-point mark. For Temple, this was a moment of elation and relief. For years he had always felt like a bit of an outsider. He lived on a different continent from most of the community. He didn't go to as many events as some of these other guys because of his location. He hadn't been in it since the 1980s, when most of these superstars first gained their fame. Despite holding the world record, there was still an air of outsider mistrust. Some had never been sure that he had actually achieved the 1,900,000 score legitimately. There was nothing that gave them any inclination that this would be true, but that didn't stop them from spreading doubt within the community:

"Is it really him playing?"

"Is he manipulating something?"

"I can't see his hands. What is he doing?"

With one quick game, he'd now eliminated any questions surrounding his legitimacy. Who could challenge what they had just seen with their own eyes? He had played a casual game on a random machine at Funspot; there was nothing he could have done to manipulate that. There wasn't any question of its qualifications to be used for a competitive score; he had achieved the impossible within the belly of the beast, and he could not have been happier. With this new record, he finally felt like he belonged.

Legendary Status: 2010

Two years removed from his impressive performance at Funspot, Tony Temple found himself yet again dissatisfied with the current state of competitive play. Since he had set the record, no one had even come close to beating him. Though he'd always been competing against himself, he felt as though he needed to up the ante and see how far he could take things.

Since starting his competitive career, he'd always wondered about the *Missile Command* kill screen. He believed it existed, but no one had ever scored high enough to actually experience it. He didn't know what it would take, but he knew he needed to be the first to hit that point.

He once again returned to the classic "start camera, fail, stop camera, repeat" routine, but found that he was making more progress than ever before, and had a clear shot at beating his 2,200,000-point record and getting closer to the ever-elusive kill screen. This is when the next evolution of Tony Temple was created. Just months after setting this goal, he hit the kill screen by reaching screen 256, scoring over 4,400,000 points and doubling his previously set world record.

When most didn't believe the kill screen actually existed, Temple persisted, knowing that at the very least he would eventually beat his high score—and that was still something to be celebrated. That's the beauty of Temple as a competitor. He doesn't need someone to challenge him in order to compete.

He's more than willing to best what he's already done in pursuit of greatness. "[It] was a goal of mine for some time," he recalls, speaking fondly of the idea to go after the fabled end game. "To be able to have gotten through that, and then to have added quite a slug of numbers on top of it, I was really pleased." As he should be. He proved something possible that most believed to be impossible, and he did it with style.

Temple was happy with what he had achieved and knew that it only further cemented his status as the best *Missile Command* player in the world. And while most recognized that and knew they could never compare, others saw it as an opportunity to take a shot at the king.

Enter Mr. Awesome

"Oh, God help us all."

In every community, there's always a villain. It might be a top competitor who everyone wants to see dethroned, it might be a cheater who ruins the integrity of the game, or it might just be someone who doesn't want to admit defeat, unable to let go. No matter who you ask in the competitive coin-op community, Roy Shildt—or Mr. Awesome, as he lovingly refers to himself— is that villain. For everything he claims to do to make the competitive community better, everyone else sees it as doing little else than causing damage and irrevocable harm.

At one point in time, Shildt—who regularly waxes poetic about all the women he gets, and who dresses up in a combination American-flag/European military outfit somehow inspired by Arnold Schwarzenegger—was the world record holder for *Missile Command* and found a deep identity in that title. It represented who he was as a person, and he wanted everyone to know it. He would attend meet-ups and harass everyone with his stories of how great he was and how everyone else sucked—

that is, until 2006, when Temple posted his 1,900,000 score, beating Shildt's score of 1,695,266 set in 1986.

With this defeat taking away the one thing Shildt held so dear, he kicked his antics into overdrive. He began attending every event possible, running around proclaiming that he was the rightful world champion. Instead of attempting to compete with Temple, Shildt opted to presume that something was wrong with Temple's run. He believed that there was no way anyone could beat him and that they must be cheating if they were able to do so—he set out doing everything he could to find out what this was. He tricked Temple, unaware of Shildt's reputation, into breaking down every component of his run so that Shildt could find something wrong with it. He started spreading rumors that there wasn't something right about it, that no one could have beaten his score out of nowhere all these years later.

Eventually he reached the conclusion that this all came down to a trackball setting. You see, throughout Atari's development of the *Missile Command* cabinet, the company ended up making changes to the cabinet's operating manual that discussed the best way to set the machine up, which was fairly common at the time. In two different versions of the manual, Atari listed different positions to have a specific switch in. This switch, when activated, decreased cursor resistance, allowing you to move the cursor at a higher rate of speed. According to the final manual, this switch should be activated, allowing for faster cursor movement. This is what Tony Temple played with, but not Roy Shildt. Shildt used the switch in the off setting, which resulted in a slower cursor, which he believes is the correct way to play, and how he set the original record.

Temple didn't know any better. He'd set everything up exactly according to how the manual instructed him, and Day didn't seem to have any instructions to do the opposite; Temple just played the game and got his score. No one would have known any different, but Shildt was determined to assert his findings as the reason that he had finally been beaten. He believed that without this setting enabled, Temple never would have been able to get anywhere near his score—thus equating Temple's use of the fast cursor as a crutch necessary to keep up with Shildt's high-level gameplay.

Despite there being two manuals, with no indication of which one was "definitive," Shildt was adamant that the game should be played with the switch in question in the off position, with the slow trackball setting, and that any other scores were invalid.

Twin Galaxies, the regulating body of competitive arcade scores, disagreed. In 2008 it issued a joint statement with Guinness World Records explaining how they were going to move forward with this, essentially presenting a solution that merged the two divergent paths into one single record accounting for both settings, allowing Temple's score to stand as the official Guinness World Record and setting the standard rules as "player's choice."

This infuriated Shildt and sent him off the deep end more than when Temple had broken his record. Due to his outlandish personality, Shildt had always been seen as a bit of a thorn in the side of the community, but some people sided with him. It essentially boils down to two camps: the first believe that Temple's settings were the most updated and therefore correct, with the second believing that, regardless of what settings were chosen, Twin Galaxies should have stepped in before awarding Temple the title and later changing the rules to fit what they had awarded. Ultimately, whichever path you believed, it never came down to being Temple's fault. He was an unfortunate pawn stuck in the middle of a much bigger battle between Roy Shildt and Walter Day. Temple had been told to play on those settings by the *Missile Command* operating manual, and that's what he had done. And it doesn't change what he accomplished.

As a result of the ruling, Shildt began finding every opportunity he could to tell the world of this injustice against him. He believed to the deepest levels of his being that he was in the right, and he wasn't going to stop until he finally got the recognition he believed he deserved. Unfortunately, as a result of this, he drove everyone away from him by going about this the wrong way. Instead of trying to win people over by explaining the situation, he became irate and attempted to make his point with loud rants that came off just one step above the worst of internet message board conspiracy theories about Area 51.

Shildt became so obsessed with proving his superiority that he tracked down Dave Theurer, demanding an explanation. Theurer, nearly thirty years after the release of the game, had no recollection of this single switch. Even if he had been asked in 1980, he wouldn't have had an opinion one way or the other. He had nothing to do with the physical production of these boards—that had all been the Atari engineering team—but that didn't stop Shildt from harassing him at every opportunity he could.

Theurer had already been haunted enough for one lifetime. He didn't need anymore of it from Shildt, and disavowed anything to do with the *Missile Command* community as a result of this experience. He would rather never touch it again than have to deal with Shildt yelling about board setting switches and how he was screwed over.

When Theurer didn't give him the answers he wanted, Shildt turned his sights on Tony Temple, the very man who had dethroned him after twenty long years. He figured that if he could get Temple to dig himself into a hole and somehow discredit himself, he could take these findings to the press and regain his title. This also did not work as planned. Temple, not really knowing who Shildt was at the time, was more than happy to share everything he knew about the game with Shildt.

Unbeknownst to Temple, the documentary *King of Kong* was being filmed at this same point in time, and featured Shildt prominently as one of Billy Mitchell's many antagonists. In the film, Mitchell's *Donkey Kong* play is challenged by up-and-comer Steve Weibe, who is laid off from his job as an engineer and dedicates his life to breaking the *Donkey Kong* world record. After much trial and error he finally does, throwing the entire competitive arcade gaming scene for a loop as this unknown player takes the crown. Mitchell, in an attempt to verify this score, sent someone to look at Weibe's machine, only to find that the cabinet's board was provided by Roy Shildt, who had vowed to enact revenge on Twin Galaxies for allowing Temple's score to stand. This immediately threw up red flags for everyone involved, leaving them to believe that Shildt had manipulated the board to trick Twin Galaxies into accepting a bad score and thus invalidate its reputation in the community. This didn't work, as any association with Shildt's name was enough for Twin Galaxies to throw out Wiebe's score for fear that it was invalid, and the plan was foiled.

This wasn't Shildt's only run-in with Day, either. At the E4All Expo in 2008, Shildt approached Day and others from Twin Galaxies with a camera, asking them why they didn't consider his scores to be valid. Day explained to him the statement they had released and his plans for updating their site to better display the differences between scores before challenging Shildt to demonstrate his skills on the machine present at the show. Shildt scored just over 800,000 points, claiming the glare made it unplayable. During this altercation, Day also explained how the lack of physical evidence—which Shildt claims Day had and purposefully destroyed to refute Shildt's score—and contradictory claims hurt Shildt's case and made his score unclassifiable.

As much as Tony Temple tried to help Roy Shildt, he was often his own worst enemy. Not knowing when to stop or how best to approach things, he often squandered any chance he had at regaining credibility within the community. In his naïveté, Temple offered multiple times to mend the bridge between Day and Shildt, but to no avail.

In August 2010 Billy Mitchell was inducted into the International Video Game Hall of Fame for his lifetime of achievements in the competitive arcade space. To show his dismay, Shildt had a Douchebag Hall of Fame plaque made, which he presented to Mitchell before being thrown out of the event.

Eventually both Walter Day and Billy Mitchell were forced to threaten restraining orders against Shildt following continued harassment and a letter from Shildt's attorney threatening an injunction from publication if they didn't recognize Shildt's *Missile Command* score as the true world record.

When Temple eventually stopped replying to him, Shildt turned to the one person he believed could help him: Howard Stern. (Yes, this is serious.) Now, during this time, Shildt did some weird stuff. Whether it was the stress of trying to prove his claims or just the need for recognition, we'll never know, but Shildt had his sights set on stardom. He wanted to become famous, no matter what the cost. In order to accomplish this, he took out a full-page nude advertisement in *Playgirl* magazine that spoke of his accomplishments as Mr. Awesome and requested people contact him for acting gigs.

According to Shildt (but entirely unconfirmed by any other source), he received many responses from some of Hollywood's biggest producers, who he claims tried to get him to engage in sex acts with them in exchange for jobs. He didn't get any jobs out of this (he claims it's because he didn't do it), but years later, on the Howard Stern show in his full Mr. Awesome getup, he claimed he had recorded everything and was in the process of selling it to Madonna (yes, *that* Madonna) for publication. (Who knows what he thought she would do with it?) Despite all indications to the contrary, Shildt thought this to be a successful opportunity to get the word out about how corrupt Walter Day, Tony Temple, and everyone else in competitive arcade gaming was. Despite making the most noise, this was perhaps the least effective method of getting to the bottom of his claims, and it left Shildt with very few options other than finding more ways to be as loud as possible.

It then became his main objective to attend these events, whether competitions or conventions, and spread his message as far and wide as he possibly could before often being asked to leave.

Schildt has created an entire series of videos using footage of Day and Temple, secretly recorded around the time of Temple's 2006 world record, that he believes devalues Temple's score, giving him back the rightful place as *Missile Command* world champion. This nearly hour-long series of videos, titled *Donkey Kong and Missile Command Conspiracy*, chronicles the transgressions that he believes were levied against him by Day, Mitchell, and Temple, as well as other members of the Twin Galaxies staff, over the course of his investigation.

Despite many accusations levied against Day and the Twin Galaxies staff over the years, Shildt's have been given very little credibility, with most chalking it up to an unfortunate circumstance and series of miscommunications that have only been amplified by a man unwilling to let go.

Roy Shildt's record was broken by Tony Temple more than a decade ago, but Shildt is more fired up than ever before. He believes every word of what he's saying and stands behind his actions fully, but won't compete on similar settings as he doesn't feel he needs to prove anything, despite his saying the version of the game that Temple played is much easier. For Shildt, the longer it festers, the more passionate he becomes about it. Tony Temple? He still loves the game more than ever.

In 2010 an additional layer was added to the controversy as pinball legend Jeff Blair passed Shildt's score with the slow trackball setting, finishing with a score of 1,874,925, surpassing Shildt's score of 1,810,630. At this point, Shildt could no longer claim even the self-imposed title of slow-settings world champion. He continued to cause a stir in the scene, claiming that due to the two variations in settings, the scores couldn't be compared, despite Blair using the same settings as Shildt. Instead, you had to take the score you were able to score by the 100-round mark, and whoever had the highest would be named world champion.

While there's some merit to the notion of a more universal scoring metric, this was yet another scheme concocted by Roy Shildt to invalidate those who had bested him and to return to his former glory. Under this new scoring method, he believed that he would outscore both Blair and Temple, who typically achieved their massive scores during the late game of *Missile Command*. Though Shildt continued to press the issue in the years following, the public now widely acknowledges Temple and Blair as the first- and second-place winners, respectively for Marathon Settings, relegating Shildt to third place.

This is just one aspect of what makes *Missile Command* so special. For decades, these guys have dedicated their lives to competing around the world in hopes of setting a record and winning the title of world champion. They've spent countless hours doing score runs and discussing the most minute details of how the game was set up, all in pursuit of a singular goal. While they undoubtedly made this choice because they were good at the game, those initial hooks of beauty, uniqueness, and difficulty made *Missile Command* an attractive package that hooked these guys in from the very start decades earlier. And while these may be extreme caricatures of the average *Missile Command* fan, it's undebatable that the effect the game had on these guys rings true as a definitive example of just how powerful Dave Theurer and Rich Adam's game had become in the minds of players.

Missile Command may have started out as a small project they just wanted to get out the door, but it blossomed into something much more meaningful. Theurer's ultimate goal was always to create something that would be powerful enough to stick around for generations—and for Blair and Temple it has done just that. They've dedicated their lives to *Missile Command*, competing and traveling the world spreading the message of their love for arcade games, and they wouldn't have it any other way.

From the Ground Up:
The Story of *Tempest*

13

I T IS SUMMERTIME, SOMETIME IN THE 1960S, AND A YOUNG DAVE Theurer is away for the summer at Patrol Camp, the annual camping tradition for his Boy Scout troop, before starting fifth grade. This was a regular trip for kids his age to make at the time if they were in the Scouts. It was a great way to learn, to complete a ton of merit badges, to hang out with your fellow troop members, and to meet new friends, all at the same time.

One night the troop decided to watch a movie together as a bonding activity. Theurer was excited; his parents didn't allow him to watch movies, so this was something special that he didn't get to do very often. Despite the massive popularity of televisions in the 1960s as they became more affordable and ubiquitous, Theurer's parents weren't on board. It was a big treat for him to be able to watch a movie with his friends, but that quickly changed when the movie started.

In the film (Theurer can't remember its title), a sinkhole opens that leads directly to the center of Earth. As the hole erupts, monsters emerge from it, attacking and killing any humans that stand in their path. For a ten-year-old who didn't watch movies, this was a formative and horrifying experience that, despite how hard he tried, he would never forget. Even years later, Theurer would find himself haunted with nightmares of this monster hole appearing somewhere near him, flooding his area with monsters who went about killing everyone he knew and loved.

Though this experience happened when he was just ten years old, these visions stuck with Theurer, reappearing in his nightmares regularly for the years following the incident. And, as we've seen, he was a man who really took this stuff to heart. Just as he wanted *Missile Command* to influence people, he knew that personal experiences could inform one's medium. He would later cite these nightmares as the basis of his work for his next title, *Tempest*.

Fast-forward to 1980. *Missile Command* has just been released, and Dave Theurer is working on prototypes for *Tempest*. Just as he had been given a prompt for *Missile Command*, *Tempest* was supposed to be "a take on first-person *Space Invaders*," which had gone on to become one of Atari's most successful games. They wanted to build off of that success and knew a change in perspective could be an interesting angle for people who had burned out on the traditional *Space Invaders*-like game.

Theurer went to work, creating working prototypes that utilized complex vector-rendering hardware that was completely groundbreaking at the time. It was still somewhat new and unproven, but once Theurer had seen it, he knew he needed to use it for *Tempest*. The clean lines fit his style perfectly and allowed him to quickly work on the concept without the need for complex art. At the time, vector systems were mostly used in computer rendering hardware, but Theurer knew that, when attached to the newly developed color vector system, they could create something that would be a sight to behold. The technology wasn't without its problems, giving him a fair share of setbacks along the way, but he found that, once again, trial and error proved to be key to his success. Within six weeks he had working prototypes up and running, ready to show off at the next Coin-Op Division meeting.

Despite extremely strong source material and a decent idea of how he thought he could accomplish this, his prototypes weren't coming together in a way that he was satisfied with. They didn't feel right, and he knew he had to find something that he could connect with before selecting that concept to build out, especially following the success of *Missile Command*. Thankfully, his work on *Missile Command* was extremely popular, so Theurer was given the time and leeway to really dive into a concept before moving on, but that didn't stop the prototyping process from becoming extremely frustrating for him. It just wasn't fun, and that ate him up inside.

He had tried multiple different iterations of the idea, but it wasn't something that he—or the internal project green-light board who give designers the approval to pursue a project—were happy with. It wasn't that they didn't like the idea—they just had a hard time believing that the general population would find it to be fun. In a business built off quarters spent in arcades, you really had to earn your money through repeat plays, and these *Tempest* prototypes didn't seem like they were all the way there.

This was a huge issue for Theurer and his team, leaving the project in a state of limbo; the team members felt like they couldn't figure it out and that the concept was becoming stagnant. In a company that moved as quickly as Atari did, producing countless games each year, stagnant and unfun were the last things you wanted to be.

Frustrated at his inability to find the defining features of the game, Theurer decided to focus on the more polished elements of what the concept could become, hoping they would inform the basic design principles they were struggling so much with at the time. As he did this, he was suddenly struck with a vision of his childhood nightmares. He recalled the fear he felt when he saw monsters erupting from a giant hole in the ground, utterly defenseless as they made their way toward him.

Theurer soon realized that he could transform the concept slightly to fit this idea. If he could find a way to take the 3-D plane and its accompanying vanishing point, he could wrap it into a cylinder that gave off the appearance of looking down into a hole in the ground. Then, just as the monsters did in the film, he could have them move up the plane toward the player's perspective, tasking them with attacking them before they could escape.

He was okay with the player being on the offense in *Tempest*. Monsters were different. He was all aboard the monster killing train, but not keen on killing people.

Filled with excitement over this revelation, he started work on this new prototype immediately, gaining the curiosity of Rich Adam, who continued to share a lab with Theurer following the conclusion of their work on *Missile Command*. Theurer quickly built out a rough framework for what this could look like and, even in the rough prototype stage, it was like nothing gamers had ever seen at the time. Heck, it even caught Adam off guard as he recalled seeing it on Theurer's monitor as he came into work one day. "Dave, what the hell are you doing?" he asked. "What is that? Where's *Space Invaders*?" He was both intrigued and shocked by what Theurer had been able to accomplish and, for Theurer, that was all the approval he needed. He knew he was on the right path.

He converted his earlier prototypes into this new design and began to recruit players from around the lab. It was an instant hit. He got exactly the feedback he was looking for with a game like this, and knew he had found the right formula. He got the approvals he needed and set off on making the rest of the game. Realizing the strength of his source material, he used what he could remember from his nightmares to fill out the rest of the game. He used them as fuel for the project, allowing them to engulf and enrapture his creativity, hoping this project might be just what he needed to banish them from his thoughts once and for all.

Just as he had with *Missile Command*, he wanted to use a unique control method that felt as though it was custom-made just for this instance. To match the cylindrical design, he settled on a knob that players could turn to quickly spin the hole to wherever the monster was attempting to escape from. It was extremely fast, just like *Missile Command*, and he knew that it was the right way to go about it. There was only one issue: he got reports that it made people sick due to the vertigo created by the speed at which the game moved.

It was a quick fix; Theurer simply changed the knob to control the player's character instead, moving around the hole rather than moving the hole itself. Once he did this, it solved all the nausea issues, and he was off to the races. He finished the game later that year, and it released in October 1981 to massive success.

This success, though exciting for Theurer, came just a few months too early, as Kassar, seeing how successful *Missile Command* had been, finally agreed to implement a bonus program that rewarded designers for games that met certain thresholds. He, unbeknownst to Theurer, wanted to see how *Tempest* performed at arcades before officially implementing the policy, costing Theurer what he believed to be "perhaps a million dollars."

There was a bright side, however. Theurer had finished another project, and the nightmares that had haunted him as a child had finally been put to good use. On the one hand, he had put to rest and buried the nightmares he had once considered to be so negative. On the other hand, he had brought these horrifying visions to public view, fully visible to all and at the forefront of his legacy. He had made his peace with them, but he worried that the ominous and unsettling monsters that adorned the cabinet art might induce the same nightmares in others—in fact, he was so worried about this that he discussed reworking the cabinet art, but ultimately left it as it was.

It was an unsettling experience. He had to pull inspiration from something so negatively powerful and let it once again consume his thoughts in order to get the result he so desired. This was all perfectly emblematic of Dave Theurer. He took the heavy ideas that were floating around in his head and internalized them, allowing himself to dive deep into the recesses of his mind in order to thrive off the dark concepts plaguing his consciousness.

As a result, he was able to deliver a visually stunning experience so uniquely different from anything else at the time that its legacy is still evident in modern games releasing decades later. For many, *Tempest* was an entirely new arcade experience. It was the first time that many realized there could be depth to a game—not metaphorically, but physically. While everyone else focused on creating something easily recognizable, he chose to do the opposite, resulting in a sensory overload experience that came to define what games could become.

The Great Crash

14

B Y THE END OF 1980 ATARI HAD BECOME THE FASTEST GROWING company in the history of the United States. Thanks to continued strong sales of its Video Computer System (VCS) and the Atari computer family, which had been introduced in 1979 and was a massive success, as well as the arcade release of *Missile Command*, Atari posted revenue of $415 million, up from $39 million just four years earlier, when Warner Communications had acquired the company and Ray Kassar had taken the helm. Warner was extremely pleased with Kassar's leadership. He had taken a money pit and turned it into a pile of gold.

Things were looking good, and Kassar believed the company was finally on its way to sorting out the problem that had been building for the last five years. The audience was finally there; they just needed to double down. Then 1981 rolled around. New arcade hits like *Tempest* took over arcades while classics like *Missile Command* and *Asteroids* made their way to the VCS. As Atari continued to grow, it was unable to keep up with the massive demand. To ensure that it could manufacture in high enough quantities for the rising demand, Atari demanded distributors purchase their inventory a year in advance, unsure that the company would be able to fill additional requests otherwise. Distributors complied, trusting that Atari's

193

success would only increase as massive blockbusters like *Pac-Man* (which Atari had licensed from Namco for release on home consoles), *Raiders of the Lost Ark*, and *E.T. the Extra-Terrestrial* were released the following year. Atari reported revenue of over $2 billion, accounting for roughly a third of Warner's total revenue for the year.

But as 1982 arrived, Atari began to face stiff competition. Its release of the VCS version of *Pac-Man* met with wide dismay. Fans had expected to receive a fully featured version of what they played in the arcade, but were treated instead to a substandard version that didn't hold a candle to the arcade version. Despite this, it did exceptionally well, eventually selling nearly eight million units. These sales came with a cost, as many felt burned, unsure of Atari's ability to compete in a rapidly growing market.

Just a month later, Activision released *Pitfall*, an adventure game that tasked players with running from screen to screen to collect treasure within a specified time limit, and that many credit as the first side-scrolling platformer. It was a huge hit, outselling every Atari release but *Pac-Man*. Around the same time, Atari finally lost its multiple ongoing lawsuits against Activision, opening the market for dozens of third-party developers to create games for the system in exchange for a royalty.

Suddenly Atari needed a real winner. Thankfully, *E.T.* was just around the corner, and everyone was counting on it to be a big hit. Atari needed the win, and distributors knew that the movie's success would help drive sales, preordering millions of copies the year before. Their hopes were quickly dashed as the game was released and considered by fans to be a massive flop. The graphics were terrible, it was hard to tell what was going on, and aimless direction left players confused as to the purpose of the game. Though it sold well at 1,500,000 copies, this fell short of the hope that everyone had for it, and consumer confidence in Atari waned even further as other games failed to sell as well as they had before.

While still successful, Atari was in a tough spot. The market had become too saturated and the company was failing to innovate, allowing itself to be overtaken by its own success, just as it almost had been in 1974 with the release of *Pong*. Now it was stuck with games people didn't want, increased competition, and little room to move forward. With the end of the year closing in, the company released the Atari 5200 in November, renaming the VCS the 2600 to signify that the 5200 was two times better than the VCS, but it was too little too late. The 5200 sold well, but on December 7, 1982, Warner Communications reported a sales increase of 10 percent, adjusted down from the 50 percent they had been boasting about, due to poor sales of Atari games. Warner stock plummeted more than 40 percent in the proceeding two days, signaling rough waters ahead for Atari. Things got worse just one week later, as the US Securities and Exchange Commission announced an investigation into Kassar and Atari vice president Dennis Groth. It was later revealed that that just twenty minutes before announcing their fourth quarter earnings, Kassar sold off five thousand shares of Warner Communications stock worth about $250,000. He claimed this was entirely unrelated, but the public remained unconvinced, as it very well should have.

Just like *Missile Command*, *E.T.* for the VCS had an urban legend of its own. In September 1983, a full year after the release, the *Alamogordo Daily News* in New Mexico reported that that more than a dozen semi trucks had picked up unsold games and systems from Atari's recently closed El Paso, Texas, warehouse and dropped them in a New Mexico landfill, never to be seen again. Atari dismissed these claims, and they fell to the wayside, doomed to the same fate as other urban legends of the time. Meanwhile, Atari reportedly sent steamrollers to crush what remained of the discarded games before encasing them in cement to ensure they would never be found. But in 2014, a documentary, *Atari: Game Over*, which profiled the crash of 1983, would unearth these cartridges, eventually finding that more than 700,000 cartridges of all kinds of Atari games had been buried after distributors returned them following poor sales.

Sales continued to plummet in 1983 as fans flocked to other home console options, unimpressed with the Atari 5200. Atari tried to recover, moving its manufacturing plants overseas to cut down on costs and increase profitability, but it was too late. Later that year, Warner reported losses of more than $283 million, largely attributed to Atari. By the end of the year, this would climb to $536 million, causing the entire gaming industry to crash around it. Atari's largest competitors reported massive losses and began laying off large portion of their workforces. In a matter of months, Kassar resigned as Warner sold off Atari to the former president of Commodore Computers, Jack Tramiel, who continued to try to save the company.

Believing the future of the company to be in computer technology, Tramiel declined Nintendo of Japan's offer to distribute their Famicom console in the US, which Nintendo would then go on to do themselves under the name Nintendo Entertainment System. Realizing the error of his ways, Tramiel attempted to pivot back to video game consoles, but competitors had already taken hold, and Atari struggled to find a foothold until eventually laying off nearly the entire company just a decade later in 1996, leaving a shell of the former company to license out the brand. It was sold to Hasbro in 1998 for $5 million.

In the span of twenty-six years, Atari had gone from a company manufacturing machines in an abandoned roller-skating rink, to more than $39 million in sales at the time of the Warner acquisition, to raking in more than $2 billion in profit in 1981, to being sold off for scraps at $5 million. There's no denying that Ray Kassar's influence over the company was extraordinary. He took a struggling business that couldn't afford to create its own product and turned it into the fastest growing company in US history. But at what cost?

The company that had once been creativity and innovation incarnate fell prey to its own success, failing to stay true to the vision that its founders set out to achieve. In an attempt to increase profits and grow to the heights that Warner hoped for, Kassar had alienated the very people who had made Atari what it was. Without that guiding foresight and thirst for innovation, the company failed to see what was headed its way, and it paid the ultimate price as a result. In spite of what ultimately became its slow and painful death, Atari's legacy lives on today through the games it created, which captivated the minds and quarters of millions of people.

Lasting Influence

15

WHILE *MISSILE COMMAND* IS WIDELY REGARDED AS ONE OF THE best and certainly most popular arcade games to have ever been released, it couldn't hold the spotlight forever. What most consider to be the golden age of arcade gaming ended in 1983, and people began to move on. The megahits like *Pac-Man* and *Space Invaders* survived, but games like *Missile Command*, which were graphically advanced at the time, were replaced by games with newer advances in visual fidelity.

Despite *Missile Command* nailing the perfectly timeless look of the 1980s and capturing it for all to remember as they look back fondly on the era, it began to feel dated as time progressed. Games moved away from line-art and toward 3-D modeling and advanced sprite (a collection of pixels that resembles a more lifelike character) work.

It was also hampered by the very control scheme that made it unique in the first place: the trackball. Though the trackball offered completely unprecedented gameplay at the time, it soon became the key to the game's downfall. People didn't want to play with a trackball when everything else used joysticks. If they were going to branch out from the traditional joystick, they wanted it to be so completely out there and unique that it felt custom-made for that title. As the machines aged, so did the trackball systems, resulting in difficult-to-repair machines with a dwindling supply of replacements. With each machine that fell victim to time, the likelihood of finding *Missile Command* at your local arcade grew smaller and smaller, until it finally became the exception rather than the rule.

Yet even as *Missile Command*'s presence in arcades began to fade, its legacy did not. Though it was understandably pushed aside for newer and more modern games, its unique and memorable gameplay had left people constantly in search of something to fill that same niche. Many games offered similar experiences, but nothing could replicate the whole package of what made *Missile Command* so special. When players couldn't find that, nostalgia kicked in.

In the years since *Missile Command*'s first release, Atari has released dozens of ports of the game, including one for the Atari 2600 in 1981. Ported by Rob Fulop, a new engineer at Atari who was fresh out of school at the University of California–Berkeley, where he earned an electrical engineering degree in 1978, *Missile Command* for the Atari 2600 was Atari's gamble at porting one of its most successful arcade titles to its new home console. It was a bit of a two-sided bet. On the one hand, *Missile Command* was extremely popular, and one of Atari's most successful titles to date at the time. On the other, it was so reliant on the trackball control scheme that there was a chance it might not work when ported to the Atari 2600's more traditional joystick. Ultimately this bet paid off, as *Missile Command* went on to be one of the best-selling titles ever for the Atari 2600, eventually landing in fourth place in sales, at 2,760,000 copies, beating out games like *Space Invaders* and *Frogger*.

In the Atari 2600 version of the game, Fulop took some liberties with the narrative that Theurer had created, adding his own backstory to the instruction manual that came with the game. In this manual he notes that the game doesn't take place in California, or even on Earth, but actually takes place in space and concerns two warring planets. In this version of the game, the enemy planet, Krytol, is at war with the player's planet, Zardon, and is launching its full arsenal of weapons upon the latter. Though this was never Theurer's intended story, and resulted in a pretty disconnected message compared to the arcade version, it ultimately didn't end up being a big deal to Theurer. Most people didn't read the manual, and were still likely to approach it as if it were taking place in a region close to them—inserting their own cities and internalizing the gameplay.

For many players, this became the primary way they played the game, even if it wasn't considered to be the best or most competitive way to do so. Through this it became clear that for most it wasn't even about the really high skill gameplay, just the experience of it all. As Theurer had always intended, fun was the first priority and, when paired with the beautiful graphics that had not been seen before that time—especially on a home console—players gravitated to it. They wanted to be able to experience the game on their own terms—as was the main benefit of the burgeoning home console movement. This holds true even today, as Atari continues to release updated ports of the original *Missile Command* on modern home consoles and mobile devices, attempting to introduce the game to new audiences that may never have experienced the earlier arcade or home console versions.

Missile Command's unique premise and stunning art direction have allowed it to stay relevant in pop culture even today. During the golden age of arcade gaming, it could be found in the most popular television shows and movies of the day, including *Fast Times at Ridgemont High* (1982) and *Terminator 2: Judgment Day* (1991), which is set in 1984 but shows kids crowded around a *Missile Command* machine, enjoying the game years after its release. It was also heavily featured in an episode of the police sitcom *Barney Miller* in 1980, in which a detective finds himself hooked on the game while trying to solve a series of crimes. Though these may be small appearances, it was still somewhat unheard of for arcade gaming to penetrate mainstream culture.

Perhaps the most notable and thorough appearance of *Missile Command* in pop culture came decades later, in 2008, with NBC's *Chuck*, in the episode "Chuck versus Tom Sawyer," which features *Missile Command* and builds off the culture that it created. The episode played on some of the fears that people had in the 1980s, with the urban legends of mind control and government interference, taking them to the next-level extremes that make Hollywood what it is. *Chuck* wasn't a stranger to incorporating gaming and pop culture content as a main plot point. In fact, most of the show revolved around these nerdy story beats. The show's main character, Chuck Bartowski, played by Zachary Levi, is the perfect incarnation of a "perpetual slacker with potential," working at the show's fictional version of Best Buy's Geek Squad, affectionately named the Buy More Nerd Herd. Chuck accidentally downloads all of the CIA's secrets into his brain, and is forced to become an undercover agent to defend the world. He's a massive gamer and nerd, so the show relies heavily on integrating these tropes into the plot. Yet very few, if any, other topics received the same treatment of an entirely dedicated episode. Though it was aimed at this aspect of popular culture, the show was fairly popular and a fan favorite for the five seasons it ran between 2007 and 2012.

In "Chuck versus Tom Sawyer" an evil crime syndicate discovers that nuclear launch codes are hidden in the kill screen of *Missile Command*, and will stop at nothing to get them. The CIA needs Chuck to stop them as they kill everyone in their path to unlocking the codes. Chuck can't do much—he isn't good enough to accomplish this—but his deadbeat coworker Jeff is. In the 1980s, Jeff was an arcade legend known for his extraordinary abilities. He's targeted by the crime syndicate, which wants to capture him to use him to break the world record for them, triggering the kill screen and unlocking the military satellites that contain the nuclear launch codes. While trying to stop them, Chuck discovers that the pattern of *Missile Command* is actually set to the beat of the song "Tom Sawyer" by the band Rush. He plays along to the song, using it to reach the kill screen and destroy the military satellite before it can be put to use by the crime syndicate. It's a doozy of an episode.

THE "CHUCK VERSUS Tom Sawyer" episode takes full advantage of the culture that *Missile Command* represents, harking back to the glory days of the golden age of arcade gaming. It perfectly captures the feel of arcades, the emotional connection that many players formed with games they were able to play expertly, and the fears that surrounded nuclear war at the time. These were all hallmarks of *Missile Command* that were so directly relatable that they formed the basis of a plot for a major television show—they were universally relatable, even if you never really thought too much about it back in the day. Despite the heavy nature of the plot, the show is a comedy, and the episode followed this comedic tone, injecting humor into something so potentially devastating and dark as nuclear war, just as Theurer had injected fun into *Missile Command* decades earlier.

It's almost perfect, the way it lines up with Theurer's message from twenty-eight years earlier. With impending nuclear doom, you must save the world and stop its destruction. There's only one major difference: Chuck saves the world; the *Missile Command* player can't. If it sounds a bit too on the nose, that's because it is—intentionally so, according to Phil Klemmer, the episode's writer.

Klemmer was a child of the 1980s and thinks fondly of his experiences growing up in that generation, consciously trying to take the lessons he learned in how he shapes his work and sees the world today. "The episode puts us in the advent of the arcade era, early to mid-eighties," explains Klemmer, noting how this also coincided with this own coming of age with gaming. "Harkening back to my childhood with the 'Star Wars' missile defense system and *WarGames*, I think all kids in the eighties grew up with this dark fascination around the idea that we could all be annihilated at any moment." He wasn't alone, either. Potential nuclear attacks were on the mind of everyone at the time, not just kids. Even President Ronald Reagan instituted the Strategic Defense Initiative, which he affectionately referred to as the Star Wars missile defense system. It was an attempt to show that the United States was developing defensive systems in outer space to protect us in the case of a nuclear attack.

"As far as video games go, [it was] pretty dark and unprecedented that you're fighting to protect the world from being annihilated by nuclear weapons," Klemmer notes. But more important than the fact that you were, was that you couldn't—the idea that no matter how well you played, you could never win really stuck with him. *Missile Command* perfectly captured this possibility and gave it real-world consequences, showing just how little would be left to care about if something like nuclear apocalypse actually happened.

The ideology fit perfectly with what they were attempting to portray in this episode of *Chuck*. Klemmer wanted to take this core belief and extend it to the plot of the show itself, furthering Theurer's intended purpose with the game. Sure, it centered around pop culture, but there were real-world consequences attached for Chuck. One little thing could go wrong, and life as he knew it would be over.

They wanted everything to match the culture that real players were experiencing in the 1980s. This is exactly why they chose Jeff, Chuck's burnout coworker, whose character as a perpetual failure and lifelong stoner made him the perfect target for the show's comedic take on a competitive arcade gamer. Flashback to 1983; Jeff is the *Missile Command* world champion. He's the exact caricature you'd expect: a flashy, neon-dressed man with women on each arm, living the life of a champion. He's essentially what everyone thought Billy Mitchell was one step away from becoming. Fast-forward to present day, and you get a very different story. Jeff's a bum, barely functioning and definitely not the best in the world at anything. Yet because of his 1983 title, the crime syndicate comes to the Buy More, trying to capture Jeff to force him to reach the kill screen for them and unlock to nuclear missile codes. Little do they know he's not exactly who he used to be, and he's certainly not who you would want as the last hope for saving (or ending) the world, but this is by design.

With avid watchers of the show having already formed their opinions of Jeff, Klemmer knew they could tell a great redemption tale. Pinning Jeff as a celebrity in the 1980s was important: he had been at the peak of intellectual performance, mastering something so well that he became an idol to many. But that was much, much different from the Jeff that everyone, including Chuck, now knew. As Klemmer points out, "the character of Jeff wasn't really good at anything. We played him as a bit of a doofus, the guy who huffed paint and took too many drugs to have more than two brain cells left in his head."

As Jeff struggles with the enormous responsibilities put upon him, he is unable to regain the skills required to accomplish this enormous feat, and it falls on Chuck's shoulders. In an attempt to figure out how to reach the kill screen, Chuck and his CIA handler Casey (portrayed by Adam Baldwin) infiltrate Atari headquarters disguised as the Nerd Herd, hoping to enlist the help of the mysterious (and fictional) creator of *Missile Command*, Mr. Morimoto. When they arrive, they find Mr. Morimoto playing the game and listening to Rush, which he claims is "the music of the universe." They soon realize it's too late, as the crime syndicate has escaped with the codes and placed a bomb on Morimoto's arcade cabinet that will explode the second he loses.

They manage to escape, but have run out of options. With no solution in sight, Chuck has to rely on his skills to get to the kill screen, but he's nowhere near skilled enough to make it happen. As he fails time and time again to perform at a competitive level, he sees a Rush shirt that triggers the information from the CIA database inside his head, finally understanding what Morimoto meant by "the music of the universe." He matches the underlying beat of the Rush song "Tom Sawyer" perfectly with the incoming rockets in *Missile Command*, finally having the solution. He throws on the song and gets to work, hitting the 2,000,000-point mark and reaching the kill screen, where he's given the code to disarm the satellite just in time, saving the real world from all-out nuclear war.

It's a fun episode that perfectly encapsulates everything that *Missile Command* is about. It meshes high-level competitive play with the fun and excitement of 1980s culture, while simultaneously addressing the urban legends of government involvement and the deeper themes of the game's narrative, all without mucking it up or making a mockery of it.

Even still, Klemmer found it to be a miracle it was ever made. Since they were a broadcast television show, they were beholden to Standards and Practices (S&P), the department at every major network that is responsible for the moral, ethical, and legal implications of anything the network airs—essentially, they're the fun police who have to worry about how things are presented, ensuring that anything broadcast won't get them in trouble. Normally, one major topic they take issue with is false information about a company that's still operational, even for fictionalized content. Yet, for some reason, they let it slide, much to Klemmer's surprise.

Nearly everything in the episode about Atari and *Missile Command* was made up for the show—not the least of which is Mr. Morimoto, who was meant more to play as a caricature of a traditional Japanese game developer rather than be accurate to Dave Theurer or Rich Adam, both of whom are white men. As a part of this, the episode also insinuates that an American company was working with the US government to hide the country's defenses within arcade games—an outlandish thought, but one that was meant to play off of the urban legends that surrounded the game at the time of its release. Due to the timely narrative of the game, many thought that Atari and the US government were working together, using *Missile Command* for a variety of secret collaborations that ranged from collecting scores for NORAD to creating a militarized version of the game for training purposes in case anything ever did happen like this and we needed to call on the best to defend us from an incoming attack.

Yet because of the widespread knowledge of these theories, S&P didn't have an issue with it. In fact, it's very likely that the ubiquity of these claims helped S&P to allow them to keep the story line in the episode. "It's *obviously* a total fabrication that the creators had anything to do with some sort of secret weapons project," explains Klemmer.

As shocked as Klemmer was that S&P didn't seem to have any issues with it, they were encouraged to proceed as long as they could get Atari to sign off on the story, which Klemmer feared would be an issue considering all of the false information they created to fit the show's plot. Yet, even more surprising, Atari was fine with it, only offering a few stipulations and asking for a mere thousand-dollar licensing fee.

These stipulations were, however, a tad confusing to the writing staff. First, they said that no one person could be portrayed as designing the game, so they couldn't say Mr. Morimoto was the sole designer. They could, however, say that he was one part of a larger team and embedded these codes without their knowledge. Oddly enough, though, Atari said that they could say all other designers were dead and that Mr. Morimoto was the only one left alive, effectively achieving the same purpose, but with a much darker tone.

Their second stipulation was that the writers could not name any other company as the creator of *Missile Command*—they didn't have to say it was Atari, but if they *did* mention a company by name, it had to be Atari. At the time the show was released, Atari was but a shell of its former self, existing almost exclusively to license off the brands it had created over the last few decades, so it made sense that the company didn't care too much and saw it as a good marketing opportunity. Their aim wasn't to make money off of the deal itself—the thousand-dollar fee was more than likely a formality to cover the costs of having to draw up the licensing agreement to hold the TV producers to their few stipulations. Even if the plot wasn't entirely accurate, it would introduce Atari and *Missile Command* to a new generation of gamers in a way that Atari never could have afforded to do at the time.

The episode's live broadcast garnered around 6.7 million viewers, and has since been made available on online streaming services, leading to the potential for millions of additional viewers.

This entire episode is a testament to the impact of Dave

Theurer's work. Klemmer could have written this however he wanted, choosing not to focus on the deeper impact of Theurer's message, but instead he took the impact that he had felt from the game and turned it into a similar message for the new generation, putting his own comedic spin on it. He was able to take the feelings that he experienced and replicate them for those who maybe didn't find the same message in Theurer's work when they had played the game decades earlier. He was able to take these common lessons and transform them to conform to modern story lines, even though the basis was still the same. That people may not be in the same mindset as they were when *Missile Command* was released in 1980 doesn't mean that the themes can't affect them. In this transformation, Klemmer created the perfect embodiment of Theurer's message and what he wanted people to understand, even if Klemmer never knew that prior to writing the episode. What he felt back in 1980 aligned perfectly with the message that Theurer wanted to share. Theurer had said that he would be content if just one person pulled this message from his work and enacted change because of it. Klemmer was this person; all these years later, the message of *Missile Command* stuck with him so profoundly that he felt compelled to share it, creating a legacy that cannot be forgotten and honoring Theurer's mission in the process.

This was all Theurer ever wanted—and *Chuck* isn't the only place the game's legacy can be found. *Missile Command* Easter eggs have been found on platforms like YouTube, in games like Bethesda's *Fallout 4*, and in television series like FX's *The Americans*.

An Easter egg is a hidden message in a work of art. For most games and movies, these come in the form of jokes or hidden references to other related content and are often hunted out by fans who meticulously scour all corners of content looking for these hidden messages. The first recorded Easter egg came from another Atari game released just before *Missile Command*, called *Adventure*. At the time of *Adventure*'s release in 1979, Atari was just beginning to find success. It had found programmers and taught them how to make games, but knew that competition was always just around the corner. Fearing that its competitors might try to steal its talent if they knew who worked on a project, Atari forbid any game from displaying credits so that the development team would remain nameless. This didn't sit too well with Warren Robinett, who wanted to be credited for his work on *Adventure*. He figured that if he couldn't outwardly put his name in there, he might as well hide it for later.

He created a panel that read, "Created by Warren Robinett." This panel would only be activated if the player brought a mysterious pixel (that fans affectionately referred to as "the dot") to a very specific room without any guidance or direction. He figured that he had hidden it well enough and that no one would ever find it, but he was wrong. Soon after the game's release, a fan wrote in explaining how he had encountered the hidden credit to Robinett and how to re-create it. Atari management was furious, and wanted affected copies recalled from consumers and replaced with noncontaminated versions. They ultimately deemed this recall to be too costly and decided to pull a 180-degree turnaround, instead encouraging their programmers to hide messages in games for their fans to find.

Since then, Easter eggs have become a ubiquitous part of gaming culture, and encountering them is often the highlight of a gaming experience for some players. These moments are unique, and really help the player feel a connection to the person behind the game.

In 2013, YouTube added an Easter egg that allowed viewers to play *Missile Command* on their web browsers, defending their video from destruction, as a part of their Geek Week celebration. During Geek Week, "geek-related content" was highlighted all across YouTube in an attempt to rally around the importance of this content to modern popular culture. To enable this, the player would type "1980" (referencing the year *Missile Command* was released) while watching a video, and the four-base clone would appear over the video player, which continued to run as you played. As the video played, missiles would rain down from above. With each hit, the video player quickly began to fill with cracks before finally breaking under the destructive power of the incoming attack. This created an interesting parallel to the original arcade release: defending what you love.

In the arcade release, this was cities and the people contained within them. In YouTube's version, it was about the content you were watching and the need to protect it, tying a direct connection back to Theurer's original purpose behind the game. This was a relatively short-lived feature, but one that many found to be a nice reminder of a game that carried with it so many fond memories of entertainment past. Where people had traditionally gone to arcades for their entertainment, they now turned to the internet.

In *Fallout 4*, players can enjoy *Atomic Command*, another *Missile Command* clone, via the interface of their in-game display named the Pip-Boy. In the game, you're surviving amid the fallout of nuclear war, which makes the inclusion a bit tongue-in-cheek, but shows the relevance of the game's message nonetheless.

In the opening of FX's *The Americans*, there's a brief shot of *Missile Command* graphics, setting the tone for the show about two Soviet KGB agents living in 1980s America. Despite there being only a brief glimpse of the game, this inclusion does much to signify the importance of the game in American culture at the time. In an era consumed with Cold War hysteria, the game's strong thematic alignment with what people were going through gave it an easy cultural touchpoint, something that most games didn't have. For most, it's associated with the Cold War, or at least the feelings of the nation at the time, so its inclusion was carefully chosen, knowing the emotions it would invoke.

These Easter eggs may be small, but they show the relevance and sense of community that remain around *Missile Command* nearly forty years later. Their relevance is a clear demonstration of just how strongly a game that's been outpaced, both technically and graphically, can still remain a popular mainstay of culture simply for being one thing: fun.

The Second Cold War

16

IT HAS BEEN MORE THAN TWENTY-FIVE YEARS SINCE THE COLD War ended in 1991. Yet for many, the feeling of uncertainty that infected countless lives during that forty-four-year face-off between the United States and the Soviet Union remains. At the time of the Cold War, it was something we faced together—you couldn't avoid it. If you were an American, there was a good chance you were fearful of nuclear war and the potential fallout that could occur if one side decided to make the first move. It was terrifying.

Though very little ever bubbled up to the surface, and often it didn't feel like a tangible war compared to other recent engagements like the Vietnam and Korean Wars, the Cold War was just as much of a concern for Americans living through it at the time. It felt like the slow burn of growing dread. Nothing had really happened, but you feared that stuff was going on behind the scenes that would eventually kick it into high gear. The silence and inaction almost made things worse, with many Americans fearing that there was action happening in the shadows, prompting them to develop a sense of paranoia and distrust that crippled the nation. We were fearful of nuclear war and knew that something had to be done, but we didn't know what, so there was a feeling that you could affect change on a local level—you could do something. Were your neighbors Soviet spies? Likely not, but that didn't stop people from jumping to those conclusions. It was an era of misdirection, and there was the fear that we simply weren't getting the whole story—there had to be more to it. Why would we allow ourselves to be threatened with something as devastating as nuclear war without cause for concern?

We weren't, but we also weren't willing to make the first move. As the Soviet Union continued to stockpile weapons (somehow unbeknownst to us at the time), the United States continued to do the same. It became an arms race to see who could collect the largest arsenal of weapons without the other knowing—"just in case." Yet as sure as we felt something might one day happen, there was also a chance that nothing ever would, that it was all posturing on the part of nations to make the whole world afraid of them. That's not something you can take a bet on, though. We had to be prepared.

In the second decade of the twenty-first century, this feeling returned, but with a new and more powerful enemy: North Korea, formally called the Democratic People's Republic of Korea.

This has its beginnings in the Korean War of the 1950s. Years before, during World War II, the United States had made it clear that it possessed nuclear weapons and was willing to use them when it dropped two atomic bombs on Nagasaki and Hiroshima. US support of South Korea and President Harry Truman's statement in a news conference that there was "active consideration" to use a nuclear weapon on North Korea made that nation fearful of an attack from the United States. As a result, North Korea went to work on developing its own nuclear weapons in case it fell under attack.

Just as with the USSR, these were less defensive and more offensive, to ensure mutual destruction, a threat that is used as a fear tactic more than anything but is terrifying all the same. The Korean War ended in 1953, but that didn't stop North Korea from continuing its work on a weapons program. If it sounds familiar, a bit like the USSR's approach, that's because the two nations were working together, even as the Cold War came to an end. By this time, the USSR was beginning to ramp down its threats and de-escalate conflict with the US, while simultaneously helping North Korea develop weapons systems in secret. As North Korea spun up nuclear reactors and threatened to use them to build nuclear weapons, the United States became more wary.

Eventually, the administration of President Bill Clinton struck a deal that required North Korea to dismantle its current nuclear operations in exchange for oil and help in building non-weaponizable nuclear energy. This timing worked out perfectly for North Korea, as it had just lost its ally, the Soviet Union, following the latter's collapse in 1991. Yet with the shift of the US presidency to George W. Bush, conflict bubbled to a head again as the president accused North Korean dictator Kim Jong-il of secretly violating the rules of their agreement and continuing to develop nuclear weapons. The US halted its side of the agreement, cutting off supplies to North Korea, which saw this as a sign of aggression and resumed work on its nuclear program.

Despite many attempts to rekindle this relationship (including two that were somewhat successful until Kim grew tired of waiting and broke the agreement, beginning to test missiles capable of delivering a nuclear payload to the United States), no real progress has been made on returning to disarmament for North Korea. There have been several times when things have looked to be on their way to being resolved, only to have one party completely flip things around when all looked to be in the clear. This has gone both ways, and in the decade following these failed attempts, things have only gotten worse, with North Korea declaring outright contempt for the United States and continuing to test nuclear weapons of escalating potency, regardless of global demands otherwise.

Just as John Milius's film *Red Dawn* had predicted the USSR to be the largest threat in 1984, and thus the main antagonist of the film, so was North Korea in the 2012 remake. In the film, North Korean soldiers invade the West Coast of the United States and a group of local kids must band together to defeat them. Though it was seen as a poor remake of a film, the second *Red Dawn* helped to cement the potential threat brewing in one of America's largest potential enemies.

In October 2014 North Korea threatened terrorist action against the United States if film distributor Columbia Pictures released *The Interview*, a comedy in which James Franco and Seth Rogen play journalists recruited by the CIA to assassinate Kim Jong-un inside North Korea. As a result, Columbia Pictures reportedly edited the film to appease North Korea, but it was still not to that nation's satisfaction.

In November of that year, Sony Pictures, Columbia Pictures' parent company, was hacked by a group that US intelligence officials believed had strong ties to North Korea, a group that calls itself the Guardians of Peace. In this hack the group penetrated Sony Pictures' confidential network, leaking emails, employee information, and even unreleased films before finally attempting to delete everything from Sony's internal network. This was a devastating cybersecurity threat that took the world by storm. The Guardians of Peace claimed they would stop with the attack if Sony Pictures indefinitely canceled the release of *The Interview*.

Sony refused, but was forced to cancel the premiere following a direct terrorist threat from the Guardians of Peace that claimed,

We will clearly show it to you at the very time and places "The Interview" be shown, including the premiere, how bitter fate those who seek fun in terror should be doomed to.

Soon all the world will see what an awful movie Sony Pictures Entertainment has made.

The world will be full of fear.

Remember the 11th of September 2001.

We recommend you to keep yourself distant from the places at that time.

(If your house is nearby, you'd better leave.)

Whatever comes in the coming days is called by the greed of Sony Pictures Entertainment.

All the world will denounce the SONY.

Following this threat, all major theater chains opted not to show the film, and Sony decided to release it online via its video-on-demand services. It grossed over $40 million in digital rentals, thus being considered a massive success. This only angered North Korea further, though the nation denied all involvement in the Sony Pictures hack.

In 2011, Seth Rogen made an appearance on *The Ellen DeGeneres Show*, where, in speaking about his wedding, he shared his love of arcade machines. As a wedding present, DeGeneres gave him an original 1980 *Missile Command* cabinet, which Rogen later referred to as the best celebrity wedding gift he had received. His love for the movie *Terminator 2: Judgment Day*, in which the game makes a brief appearance, earned the game "a special place in [his] heart." The cabinet now resides in his home in Los Angeles.

In 2017, US president Donald Trump antagonized North Korean Dictator Kim Jong-un by calling him Rocket Man and saying he was "on a suicide mission." This angered Kim, who said that Trump "would pay dearly" for these accusations, that he was "mentally deranged," and that his actions only solidified Kim's belief that America was an enemy.

This ongoing war of words between Trump and Kim echoes what Americans were experiencing during the Cold War— threat for threat, fear for fear. Only now, the escapism is gone. In 1980 you could get away from the news for a while—it wasn't all-consuming, as you only had limited sources for how you could hear about new developments. The internet as we know it didn't exist, the twenty-four-hour news cycle was only in its infancy, and you certainly didn't have a president tweeting about other world leaders at 2:00 a.m.

We found ourselves in another standoff, experiencing the same fearful, haunting uncertainty that comes with nuclear war. One day you could be sitting at your child's baseball game, the next there's nothing left of what once was downtown Los Angeles. The times that we once thought were over, never to return again, are back, and more powerful than ever. Held in a state of collective captivity, we are once again in a place where we're affected by the ever-looming threat of mutually assured destruction that comes from flirting with nuclear war.

This was the world that Theurer predicted would come about. He knew that if we changed nothing, the Cold War would go on forever, whether with the Soviet Union or another new enemy. He didn't see a world in which we would be able to continue to live knowing this was always a potential option. His message was a prediction of the future if we didn't enact change and recognize the position we were getting ourselves into. As we continue to experience similar events, we're finding out just how true his message really was.

The notion that, more than thirty years later, we haven't learned our lesson and continue to fall into the same traps that we did then terrifies Theurer. "The nightmares have left," he says, speaking of the horrific visions he experienced while working on the game. "However, I'm still haunted when I think about atomic bombs being controlled by North Korea and Iran, and by rogue terrorists." In his eyes, something must be done, as we cannot live through another extended period of this turmoil.

Though we may be more than thirty years removed from the game, we need *Missile Command* more than ever. We need the game's heart. We need the game's message. We need someone like Dave Theurer.

17

Defining a New Generation of Games

WHEN I THINK ABOUT WHAT DAVE THEURER ATTEMPTED TO AC-complish with the design of *Missile Command*, I think of art in its highest form. Art is about giving viewers something to attach to, something to connect with if they so choose. But they don't have to connect with it if they don't want to; they can just enjoy the game for what it is—a game. Just like a Rembrandt painting, you can dive deeper into the meaning of what he was feeling at the time he painted it, or you can simply think it's a nice painting. It's up to you. That subjective nature is what sets something aside from being an objective creation into a cultural touchstone that can be interpreted however you choose.

The creation of *Missile Command* was filled with risks—everything from the trackball to the defensive nature of the game. It was all stuff that hadn't been done before and, potentially, could have never been done again. It was inspiring in a way that games hadn't really been up to that point. It tasked players with some really heavy themes, knowing perfectly well they could do nothing to keep the inevitable from occurring. It knew the type of message it was trying to send, even if each and every player didn't. And that was okay; Theurer wasn't trying to connect with every player, just the few who needed it most.

At the time that *Missile Command* was released, people weren't able to break the mold and do something out of the ordinary, mainly because no mold or sense of ordinary had been established. It was still the Wild West in terms of what was acceptable in gaming—but, perhaps even more than game developers are today, they were beholden to the whims of the almighty quarter. As a programmer in such a new and underdeveloped industry, you lived and died by how your game sold; you didn't get many chances to establish a track record. At the scale that Atari was producing these games, you couldn't afford any flops—a single *Missile Command* cabinet cost $871 alone for Atari to make (not including labor), which, at the end of its lifespan, amounted to nearly $14.2 million in production costs alone. But they were willing to take those risks anyway. Dave Theurer and Rich Adam believed in the gameplay and the message; ensuring that players were able to experience both of those was worth potentially blowing their shot at a megahit.

In doing so, they were able to break through what players had come to expect from early arcade games and to give them something special. Though players had come to simply burn a quarter on some simple gameplay or pretty graphics, they were instead treated to something they hadn't seen before, and this opened them up to the possibilities that came with an entirely new experience. When most games had black-and-white graphics, *Missile Command* had vibrant, beautiful colors. When most games used simple joysticks, *Missile Command* used a trackball to allow for greater control fidelity, making the game faster and more challenging. When most games started off easy and became more challenging after a while so that you felt your quarter was well spent, *Missile Command* was brutally difficult. It never felt unfair, and gave you a few rounds to warm up, but if you didn't have an expert level of precision over that trackball, it wasn't going to be something you could plan on playing for a while. You were toast.

Missile Command showed what was possible from a game, exploring uncharted and innovative territory that many thought to be impractical. It showed others at Atari that you could take risks and still find success, even if that meant that not everyone was perfect from the get-go, and you needed to make some changes along the way. It showed players that stepping outside their comfort zone to play something different might offer a long-term reward unlike anything they'd previously gotten from an arcade game.

Missile Command's famous game ending, which showed a massive explosion filling the entire screen with the overwhelming blast of a nuclear bomb, became one of its most defining features. It was a small touch, but helped to drive home the severity of what had just occurred. Nuclear war wasn't the walk in the park the game made it seem to be. It was disastrous, and ended with the same results regardless of how well you played. This was the result of a simple office exchange that occurred between Theurer and his boss, Steve Calfee.

Theurer had figured out how to make the large explosion appear following a loss. He thought it was a nice touch, but Calfee found the secret sauce. Walking by, he said, "You should have it say THE END instead of GAME OVER. It's much better." And with that simple exchange, Theurer's ultimate vision was complete.

All of this has allowed *Missile Command* to create a lasting legacy and hold a spot in the list of most well-known and memorable video game titles, almost forty years after its release. It was initially a game created for a specific time and place, but based on the world we live in today, it's turned out to have a timeless message for a struggling generation. The current generation wasn't around for the Cold War. They didn't live through the struggle and see its resolution. They know the uncertainty and fear that comes with such a scenario, but only because they're living through that same scenario with a different opponent right now. *Missile Command* has remained relevant because of nostalgia for its impressive and captivating graphics and its demanding and riveting gameplay, but now the game is more relevant than ever because its message has resurfaced just when it's needed most. This is the beauty of *Missile Command*: though the message was meant for 1980, it's relevant for 2018 and beyond. As long as we perpetuate arms races and allow ourselves to compete in a never-ending battle for supremacy, we end up doing nothing but holding ourselves hostage and succumbing to fear-inciting terrorists who want nothing more than for us to act, knowing we may well destroy ourselves in the process.

Theurer's original belief was that for us to break the nuclear cycle, we must first acknowledge the situation in which we find ourselves, to realize we're engaged in a losing battle and do everything we can to escape it. This isn't as easy as it sounds, but Theurer wasn't expecting everyone in the world to drop their arms and come together to sing John Lennon's "Imagine" simply because they had played a game of *Missile Command*. He wanted to inspire, but only if it was productive for furthering the goal of moving us away from the dangerous real-life nuclear game. Despite the strong heroic and nationalistic tones of *Missile Command*, he didn't want anything to do with inspiring anyone to continue farther down the same path, even if they believed it was for the betterment and defense of their country.

He wanted nothing more than for people to be affected by the game's message. Too many times he'd seen the nuclear powers come close to reaching an agreement, only to let politics and egos get in the way. He wanted forward progress, and was willing to sacrifice everything he had, including his sanity, to make it a reality. If even one person was affected enough to enact a 1 percent change toward stopping the proliferation of nuclear weapons, that would be a success for him.

The screen message of THE END, rather than GAME OVER, was perfectly clear: you didn't just lose, you and everything you loved was annihilated. There were no extra lives; there were no do-overs. Once we go down this path, there's no coming back, and nothing will ever be the same no matter which side of the engagement you're on. This lack of a way out was the entire crux of Theurer's argument: in nuclear war, there are no winners.

18

"Do You Feel Like a Hero Yet?"

L OOKING BACK, IT'S EASY TO FORGET THAT WITH ALL THE ADVANCES in gaming over the last few decades, games didn't have much in the way of story in 1980. In fact, most weren't much more than, "Enemies have appeared. If you a press a button, you shoot. You should probably shoot those enemies." They were technical marvels, and we were happy to be playing them, but the story behind the gameplay left something to be desired, even if that wasn't the reason you sat down to play in the first place.

These narratives, if made at all, were often relegated to a position outside the gameplay itself, explained in a quick paragraph of text somewhere on the arcade cabinet. At least they were trying, but few read these attempts at a story, and they certainly didn't have an impact on how players experienced the game.

That wasn't enough for Theurer, though. He didn't want to just create another black-and-white adventure game that required you to shoot at an incoming enemy until you saw the game over screen. He wanted you to take something from the experience—he wanted you to leave with a message—a *real* message— even if he couldn't tell it as deeply as he wanted to through the game. He captured the overwhelming fear of society at the time and used it as the vehicle for his message. If he was able to get people to associate their feelings with what they were experiencing in the game, he might be able to share his message without heavy-handedly forcing it into the game. He didn't want the narrative to overwhelm the gameplay, and he wasn't going to let what most would enjoy suffer for something a few might find interesting. But he also wasn't ready to let it go entirely.

Game narratives are common now, almost required. You don't see many modern games released without at least some semblance of a story thrown together to help justify the players' actions and the scenarios they find themselves in. Many are garbage, and serve as little more than filler, but some stand out as exceptional.

Others take things one step further, utilizing the same technique as Theurer to pressure the player to explore more meaningful narratives outside of what's meant for the general audience. *Spec Ops: The Line*, released in 2012 by 2K Games, is a perfect example of a dark and intense player narrative in modern gaming.

On the surface, it appears to be another military shooter, a genre that had become overwhelmingly synonymous with gaming in the early twenty-first century; and it is, but beneath its exterior you realize there's something more to it. Most games that fall into this camp tend to focus on making everything big; you must save the world, nukes are going off, and so on. Everything is purposefully detached from who the character is. They don't want people to be able to relate on a personal level, they want the faceless hero to be stripped down to "Well, they're human" levels of relatability. And that's fine, but that's not *Spec Ops: The Line*.

As the game's writer, Walt Williams, explains, *Spec Ops* is meant to be personal. He wants you to be able to relate to the soldiers in the game, whether you've ever seen a moment of combat or not. He wants you to feel their struggles, to understand their pain, and to be forced to remember that they aren't just soldiers, they're humans. As Williams told Greg Miller on IGN's *Up at Noon* around the time of the game's release, he wanted to create a game that "was actually about the soldiers that were going into combat [and] what happens when you take men and you put them into an increasingly bad situation until eventually they start to break." He wanted it to be an opportunity for players to explore the more personal side of games that so typically attempt to withdraw all human elements from gaming.

In the game, Dubai is destroyed by a series of catastrophic sandstorms that require American troops, including Colonel John Konrad and his "Damned" 33rd Infantry Battalion, to enter and help with evacuations. Unfortunately, these evacuations never happen, as Konrad and the entire Damned 33rd desert, declaring martial law and taking over Dubai, cutting off all communication. Captain Martin Walker (which is your role as game player) is sent in with two other members of Delta Squad, a US Army special forces unit, to verify the existence of a group of survivors fighting back against the Damned 33rd and figure out what's going on. But upon arrival they quickly realize that nothing is as it seems. Though originally this was meant to be just a fact-finding mission, Walker can't help himself; he sees the atrocities being committed by the 33rd and has to step in. Once engaged, Konrad and the 33rd know of Walker and his men, and they tempt them into continued engagement.

Tracking Konrad's squad to a specific area, Walker realizes they're outnumbered and makes the call to use weaponized white phosphorus, a deadly chemical agent, on the group. Presented with the horrors of what this agent could do, Walker is questioned by his squad, saying they could go about it another way, that "there's always a choice," to which Walker coldly replies, "No, there's not," before setting up a mortar launcher to start raining down destruction on Konrad's army. This sequence, presented in a top-down thermal viewpoint, is different from everything you, the player, have encountered thus far in the game. You're put in a position of absolute power, taking out multiple enemies at once without even having to expose yourself. In the reflection of the targeting computer, you see Walker's face, stoic, unaffected by the destruction at hand. Walker soon finds out, however, that that wasn't Konrad's army at all; it was a group of refugees escaping from Konrad's clutches. He breaks down, realizing the atrocity he has just committed: in an attempt to defeat Konrad and save the civilians, he has instead killed dozens of the civilians, making him just as bad as Konrad. He's been misled; Konrad purposefully tricked him into attacking the civilians. "We were helping," whimpers one of the phosphorous victims with his final dying breath, looking directly at Walker, who believed himself to be doing the same.

As the next level loads, the game taunts you with subtle new loading screen text: "Do you feel like a hero yet?"

At this moment, you think about the effect you're actually having on the situation. Are you making it any better? You just killed a few dozen innocent civilians, but it was an accident, or at least that's what you tell yourself. While you may have entered with the best of intentions, each subsequent choice in the battlefield has an effect on the core of who Walker—and by extension, you, the player—is. Unlike other military shooters, the game forces you to feel the gravity behind each and every choice you make, slowing causing you to think "Maybe this isn't the best way to go about this" despite your continuing contradictory actions otherwise.

Williams wanted players to think about this in a few different ways, beyond just gameplay. Undoubtedly, most players were initially drawn to *Spec Ops* for its unique sand environment setting and the gameplay that it provided, and not really for the narrative—he knew that going into it. It was an interesting setup for a story, but until the player got into the thick of it, it could easily be perceived as just another one of the military shooting games it was trying so hard to distinguish itself from. Because of this, Williams and the other developers knew they had to figure out how to use gameplay as a narrative lever for the player rather than for the game.

Spec Ops: The Line starts off like most modern action games: a cutscene setting up the basic backstory, shooting some guys, another cutscene that gets to the real meat of what you're going to be experiencing, shooting some more guys, and repeat. But as you progress through the story, the game itself begins to turn, slowly transitioning from basic shooter into a much more thoughtful exploration of choice, morality, and obsession, questioning your actions as you progress. The game doesn't get in your face; if you didn't know any better, you'd never notice, but the farther into the game you make it, the more Williams's challenge to the player begins to surface. It might start innocently enough as you're forced to decide between killing two people, both of whom did something horrible. No matter which you choose, nothing changes in the story; you'll get the same outcome. But the idea is that the consequences of choices don't necessarily have to be reflected in the game to have an effect on the player. As the player you might not realize it, but the next time you encounter a similar choice, you will be confronted with your original decision and how that might factor in to what you're about to do.

Williams wanted players to realize that in war there are no good or bad decisions—only decisions with different trade-offs. Sometimes you might have to take the least awful option, knowing full well that it isn't ideal, or make a choice without being able to fully think through all the possible repercussions, forcing you to live with the consequences of that split-second choice. It isn't about creating a game that branches off into eighteen different directions with each choice, but about using the player's branching emotional state to have the same effect. If you chose to execute the enemy and take their ammunition and supplies, it might have been worth it, but you might also be horrified in the process, changing the way you'll approach that scenario the next time you encounter it. Just as with *Missile Command*, Williams didn't want the message to be shoved down players' throats, but rather for it to be a subconscious one that players could interact with if they chose to. At the end of the day, some people might not have treated the game any differently from the average *Call of Duty* title, and that was okay. But for those who did, Williams wanted there to be great meaning.

As you progress through the game, you begin to question your choices—as does Walker, wondering if it is all for naught. Things go south pretty quickly, and throughout the course of the campaign, Walker is forced to choose among many different paths, none of which are objectively right, and thus to live with the horrifying consequences. These consequences begin to take a toll on him mentally as he begins to hallucinate, causing him to question his sanity. At the same time, these hallucinations are causing you, the player, to question what you're seeing: Was that real? Did I actually kill that guy? Am I really here? This collective mistrust of what you're experiencing grows deeper the closer Walker gets to Konrad. By the time he finally confronts him at the end of the game, Walker is a broken man, barely able to stand, and in the tattered rags of what were once high-end tactical gear. He's been through hell, having seen and done things he'd never thought possible, and is ready to make someone pay for it.

Yet upon arrival, he finds nothing but Konrad's rotting corpse with a self-inflicted bullet to the head from long before

Walker and his team arrived. He's then faced with the reality that Konrad was never really there to begin with. When they landed, they had encountered a local militia, and the release of the white phosphorus had messed with Walker's brain, causing him to have horrendous hallucinations. In reality, he was the one who had carried out all those actions, committing the very atrocities that his traumatized mind had convinced him were Konrad's doing. He was his own worst enemy; he was Konrad. You, the player, are then faced with the only true game-altering choice based on gameplay where your in-game actions have direct consequences on how your specific story progresses: with both Walker and Konrad at gunpoint, how do you proceed? There are two ways this can play out. Each choice results in a unique outcome and is the accumulation of every moral choice you've made thus far.

Knowing all that you've done, do you let Walker live? Was he justified in his actions against Konrad, whom he believed was the true perpetuator of these crimes, or was he the real menace all along? Or are both true?

With this choice, the game is essentially saying, "You've done all this stuff. It was you. How would you deal with someone who did what you did?" It forces you to choose your own fate. Walker hadn't started off with a choice to be bad—and neither had you. Walker came to Dubai in the hopes of saving those who others couldn't, despite knowing the odds. But in the end, he made choices, and needs to face the consequences, which was ultimately the message that Williams wanted to share. We often start with good intentions, simply playing through a game, not associating our character's actions with our own. But as we continue to make choices, it becomes clear that the two are intertwined, and our merged situation evolves in ways we aren't always cognizant of at the time, something Williams refers to as not "moving through the darkness rather than being engulfed by [it]." As a result of this intertwined narrative with Walker, you must determine your own fate, asking yourself, "Do you feel like a hero yet?"

If you allow Konrad to kill Walker or the manifestation of Konrad inside his head to kill himself, the game ends with the two corpses side by side, Walker having succumbed to the immense sorrow of his actions and unable to continue living. Fade to black. If you choose to kill Konrad, Walker lives to see another day, pushing off the moral resolution of what he did. He radios in for help, ready to go home. US Army forces arrive, ready for evacuation, but the game isn't done making you choose. In a twist, there's another gameplay-based choice in the epilogue. Walker approaches the troops wearing Konrad's jacket and carrying a weapon. They tell him to drop it, unsure of his intent. At this point, you have two options: drop the weapon or open fire. If you drop the weapon, the game ends with Walker riding off into the sunset with the troops. One turns to him, telling him of the devastation in the city, and asks, "How'd you survive all this?" Walker replies, "Who said I did?"

If, on the other hand, you choose to open fire, it ends one of two ways: you die in a pool of your own blood or you defeat the platoon, informing the rest of the troops that they're going to have to go through you with the same ominous opener that Konrad told Walker at the beginning of the game: "Gentlemen, welcome to Dubai."

There are no good or bad endings, just as there are no good or bad choices. There are only choices formed through your experiences, and you must live with them. This message is powerful, especially in an industry filled with shooter games that often try to detach players as much as possible from their actions. And yet the message is one that can only be accomplished through gaming. If *Spec Ops* were a film, you would be removed from it. "It was them, not me," you'd say. But in video game form, it wasn't just them. Every consequence that came from the game happened because of something you did, whether you realized it or not at the time.

In one final "take that" showing there truly are no good endings, Walkers' ride home after surrendering fades to white, not black. According to Williams's story, every instance in which the game fades to white is the delusional manifestation of Konrad within Walker's mind, showing that, even in the one that seems "kinda okay," he never truly found peace. It was all in his head.

Just as Theurer had done more than thirty years earlier, Williams gave players more than they were asking for. He'd given them a result they were directly responsible for. The game doesn't leave you with a sense of accomplishment at the end. Instead, it's nothing more than a sigh of relief that it is finally over—at least for you. There was no way to truly "win" the game. Each option defies traditional game endings, leaving the responsibility on you, the player, to figure out where to apply the lessons that have just unfolded before you. In reality, most players leave with nothing other than the feeling of "Wow, that was a tough ending!" But for some it was a closer look at just how quickly things can spiral dangerously out of control, into situations where we don't even recognize ourselves anymore.

This is just one example of the narrative style that Theurer developed, paving the way for games to be used as an artistic medium, and it perfectly demonstrates the power that this type of narrative can have when created with care. It isn't just an interesting story; it is a commentary on the culture of gaming and the player's actions within the game itself. In a time when almost every game had the average player gunning down thousands of enemies all in the pursuit of something "good," *Spec Ops* broke the mold, showing that *everything* has consequences—seen or not. It wasn't intended to sell more copies or appease a mass audience; rather, Williams felt the story needed to be told, and he found the only medium that would let him tell that story. As a result, he was able to create a game that so perfectly encapsulated the culture of gaming at the time, melding the player and character narratives together while simultaneously allowing one to mislead the other, causing both to question which was reality in a world where every action has a cost.

Pioneering the Future

19

E VEN TODAY, THERE MIGHT BE SOME OF YOU WHO HAVE NEVER played *Missile Command* in its original arcade cabinet form but are familiar with the game because of its appearances in popular culture, perhaps as Easter eggs in movies or YouTube videos, or as releases of the game on home consoles over the years. It might have been the bright, colorful visuals, or it might have been the blisteringly fast gameplay, which today's games just can't match, but many people familiar with gaming culture at some point in the last few decades have been drawn to *Missile Command* at one point or another. It doesn't matter if you're five or fifty; the game is accessible to anyone, breaking through age and cultural barriers. Dave Theurer's message transcended generations and found a way to live on far beyond the cabinet that once contained it decades ago. Even as interest in arcade games has diminished as mobile gaming, next-generation internet-connected consoles, and virtual reality have taken over as the gaming media of choice for a new generation of gamers, *Missile Command* has maintained its presence and position as an undeniable staple of gaming past.

Just as games were cycled out for newer, more advanced titles when they were no longer popular in arcades, gaming has evolved to a place where most games don't stick around for more than a few weeks. You might find an online gaming community you can really sink your teeth into and stretch that out to a few months, maybe even a year, but for the most part, games aren't meant to be long-term commitments. They're made in a way where content is meant to be consumed and discarded. The game developers already have your sixty dollars; why should they need to keep you entertained years later? Now, with widespread use of the internet, there are definitely some games that have found a way to stand the test of time, with MMOs (massively multiplayer online games) like *World of Warcraft* and long-standing franchises like *Halo* and *Uncharted* stretching their existence out over several iterations to ensure that they're always delivering exactly what their fans are looking for. But you no longer have to create one thing that can be replayable for as long as the game exists. You can choose to update the content later, changing certain elements around, or even turn it into a whole new game.

Games are no longer fighting for a player's money one quarter at a time like they once were, but as technology has advanced, we've been given something much more meaningful in exchange. These leaps forward in what's possible have allowed us to tell much deeper stories within games than when *Missile Command* was being developed in 1979. Though it was one of the first titles to really tell a story, that didn't mean much for most players. They knew what they were experiencing, but it wasn't as easy to put it all together in their head. Developers were reliant on the players to figure it out themselves, especially when it came to arcade titles that weren't in an ideal environment for reading through line after line of text to get a backstory. Since games were so new, it didn't really matter. In the golden era of arcade gaming, there was so much experimentation happening that players were more focused on what was new and exciting rather than diving really deep into any one game. It wasn't like you paid for a cabinet and took it home. If you didn't connect with a game, you'd simply not give it another quarter and move to the next machine; no harm, no foul.

Just as there were people calling games nothing but a waste of time, there were plenty of people on the other side saying back then that games were going to be the next major art form. I don't blame a single person for being skeptical when movies and books were so direct with their plots. Then again, a painting doesn't tell you how to feel about it. It simply exists and lets you handle the rest. This was the style that most arcade games followed at the time. They wanted to do more, but were competing for limited attention in a suboptimal environment. It wasn't ideal, but that was okay. It allowed players to create their own stories, which was much easier to connect with than trying to understand a deeper narrative when they really only cared about getting that high score.

Arcades were quick, high-energy places. If you connected with a machine, you could find yourself there for hours, but you still probably said to yourself, "Hmm, I wonder why this frog is trying to cross such a busy road in the first place." This began to change with the popularization of home consoles, as developers and players alike started to realize how important the story could become to the success of the medium. It was no longer about short sessions, and gaming began to shift away from low-variance, high-replayability titles. Players didn't want something so fast in this environment; they wanted to spend hours working toward a singular goal. Now that they didn't have to worry about anyone kicking them off the games (because they were on their own televisions), players wanted to save that princess for real—it became less about high scores and more about actually winning. While it was once good enough to beat their friends and hold the high score, they were now battling against the game itself, fighting for absolute dominance.

Yet as this shift occurred, forcing many games to become nothing more than remnants of the past, *Missile Command* was still there. It resonated with players, standing the test of time, just as its creator Dave Theurer had intended, even when similar games fell by the wayside. Others had focused on gimmicks that played well at the arcade but were quickly outpaced by technological innovations. One week yours was the only game in the arcade with a steering wheel, but the next week something new came in that was different, and you were left out in the cold, wishing gameplay had been more of a priority. As with anything, there are always winners and losers—more the latter than the former in the arcade business—but Theurer had done everything he possibly could to keep *Missile Command* from falling prey to the losing fate. He and his team at Atari were doing everything right with a color monitor, a unique concept, and a new control method, but Theurer knew that this wouldn't be enough for the game to reach its full potential, or to create the legacy he so daerly wanted for it. The game's message was important: he knew that nothing would be worse than pouring himself so heavily into a project only to have it fade out of consciousness when the hottest new game came out.

Theurer's creation needed gameplay that players couldn't get anywhere else—and that's exactly what ended up setting *Missile Command* apart in the long run. It looked pretty, and it was fun to use the trackball, but none of that would matter if the game wasn't fun to play. And yet, nearly forty years later, *Missile Command* is as popular as ever, a fan favorite in the resurgent "barcade" community. It had done its job back in 1980, pushing players to the upper limits of their playing ability, with memorable and terrifying gameplay that entered the American consciousness just when it was needed most. Nuclear war was everywhere, but the threats had been there for so long that many forgot just how powerful of a predicament we'd found ourselves in. Though that threat may have passed (even as a new one has entered), that feeling can't easily be shaken, and a strong lust for the vibrant culture of the 1980s has allowed that nostalgia to return with *Missile Command* in the driver's seat. Stumbling across it in a bar, emotions come flooding back. What had been such a fun experience during a horrifying time was now allowed to stand alone, absent from the implications it brought with it at the time. Instead of it being a horrifying reminder of how close we came to nuclear disaster, players are treated to that memory of fun, asking themselves, "Do I still have it?" with a smile, clutching a pint.

Though arcades have been declining since the late 1980s, there's still a large appetite from gamers who grew up during the golden era of arcade gaming to experience the classics they once dumped their entire allowances into. This has manifested in the form of arcade bars—including the originator, Barcade—that began to take hold in the early 2000s and have been exploding in popularity, with hundreds of iterations popping up all over the United States. These aptly named establishments often feature some of the largest selections of classic arcade games in the area, and their bar business allows them to fund an otherwise declining market. For many gamers who don't have the dedication or patience that Tony Temple does, arcade bars are the best way to get a group of friends together and relive the days of old with a few rounds of *Missile Command* and a beer in hand. In fact, they have become so popular that they've started a resurgence in arcade gaming culture as a whole, resulting in the development of new arcade games, like *Killer Queen*, specifically catered to party-like atmospheres.

Dave Theurer stepped away from games in search of something different. He said his piece and made the games he wanted to make—he was good without continuing to force his ideals. He wanted to open the eyes of those who needed it most and find solace in others who resonated with his beliefs, and he did just that. He took a chance on his dreams to break the mold of what was being done at the time, pushing others to continue to follow his path even after his time in the industry was done. It's been decades since the Cold War ended, but the saying "Those who do not learn history are doomed to repeat it" has never rung more true. Theurer created something so genuine that, despite its creation for a very specific point in time, it's just as relevant as ever.

As an industry, video gaming does a great job of recognizing forward-facing talent, but often misses out on some of the most powerful and artistic creators simply due to the scale of people required to make games actually happen. Theurer's sole accolade within the industry sums up his contributions nicely: he was a *pioneer*. He wanted to create things that were fun, but he wanted to push the industry forward while doing so. He wanted to leave his mark through the games he created, not because he was screaming the loudest.

Through the creation of these legendary games, Theurer found his creative output. He was lucky for this to occur when it did—he thrived on Atari's open culture, which he classified as "a rich environment to freely explore ideas and develop new games," when talking about Atari in his Pioneer Award acceptance speech at the 2012 Game Developers Conference. He was a man on a mission, serving as a reincarnation of Nolan Bushnell's original vision for what he wanted Atari to be focused on: fun and innovation.

In each one of his projects, Theurer pushed the envelope, looking to improve on what was commonplace at the time. Most games were monochromatic; he'd make the game full color. Most games used a joystick; he'd use a trackball. Most games were two-dimensional; he'd find a way to make the first 3-D game. Without these innovations, there was nothing to distinguish Theurer and his team from the dozens of other game developers creating arcade titles at the time. He wanted always to raise the bar, using his own work to show other game developers what was possible, even if it didn't always appear to be at first.

Without the dual principles of fun and innovation, Theurer believed that there wasn't much left to gaming. If you focused on the two of those, everything else would fall in line. It's somewhat ironic that narrative isn't one of those principles considering the importance he put on the message of *Missile Command*, but the game's success is proof enough of the truth in this mission statement.

When I interviewed him for this book, Theurer had one chief concern. He was scared; scared that, for as much as these games had haunted him, they might have the same effect on others. He had gone through such a powerful and challenging time that he had no choice but to fully remove himself from it later on. He lives a different life now, one without the fear that comes with nuclear war. He has kids and a quiet life; prior to my contacting him, he hadn't discussed the game in years, and didn't want his kids to think that he was any less a person for having experienced what he had during the creation of *Missile Command*. He didn't care how he looked to everyone else. As with everything he did, he just wanted to ensure that he didn't cause anyone else harm in the process.

In this I saw the Dave Theurer who made *Missile Command*, the Theurer who wanted nothing more than to create a better world for those around him. I saw a man whose selfless actions haunted him, and the man who hoped others wouldn't have to experience the same nightmares he did. I saw a father who wanted nothing more than to create the best possible world for his children, and their children, and their children's children.

Looking back on it, I think he did just that. Through *Missile Command* he taught a generation that war is not the answer, that there are other avenues of survival. Through *Tempest* he showed players that they could defeat their greatest fears no matter what form they came in. Through his actions, he taught me what it meant to be a creator, a protector, and a teacher. His impact on this industry is immeasurable, and we are in his debt for the spirit of innovation, relentless passion, and ability to do what's best for the player.

Spec Ops: The Line asks us, "Do you feel like a hero now?" I would say that such a word isn't strong enough to characterize Dave Theurer.

MORE THAN THIRTY years after the release of both *Missile Command* and *Tempest*, Theurer would reflect on his accomplishments during his acceptance speech for the Pioneer Award in 2012, calling Atari a "dream environment." Atari had been a place that allowed his creativity to thrive without the concerns that usually come within large companies. Despite Atari's move toward becoming more formal and corporate, he felt it was a world free from bureaucracy and politics—unlike anything he's found since.

Despite his complaints about the bonus program, Theurer was never in it for the money. Ever since he first played *Pong* in 1974, he had been captivated by the idea of creating a game so fun that people wouldn't want to stop playing. He wanted to create something enjoyable, refined just to the point where you felt as if you could play forever if there was a way to do so.

He knew this would be tough to accomplish, but he put in the work, playing "the game over and over thousands of times myself," through which he was able to find the best way to "smooth out the gameplay, eliminate the boring parts, and add surprising elements to keep things exciting." This was the basis for all of Theurer's creations—awe and excitement around every corner. He didn't know the best way to make a game—no one did—but he knew the best way to make games that he would want to play, and he hoped everyone else would feel the same way. Solutions weren't always evident, and they required endless trial and error, but "at some point, I would *feel* the right thing to do, almost reflexively."

Though he eventually left the gaming industry, he looks back fondly on his time at Atari, calling the process "the most productive and fulfilling that I've experienced in my career." He's moved on, he's focusing on other things, but his passion for innovation and the industry he helped to create remains just as strong as it was in 1980.

Ralph Baer is often referred to as the father of video games, with Nolan Bushnell earning the title of the father of arcade games. Others came before and many more came after, but Theurer's impact has rarely been replicated. He innovated, doing what many believed to be impossible, pushing the boundaries of what had been done before in the pursuit of excitement. He taught us that games didn't have to be simple sports clones focused on replicating reality, but could instead be a vision of what's to come. He also shared his message, showing that games didn't need to be focused exclusively on entertainment, but could double as a commentary on the state of the world at the time—thus proving that the debate for games as art doesn't rely solely on their sensory qualities. But, most important, he gave us diversion when we needed it most.

He might not go down in history as the father of modern gaming, but he most certainly will as the cool uncle whose crazy ideas and wild passion for fun inspired the next generation to break the mold and do something great.

Epilogue

THOUGH ITS PHYSICAL PRESENCE MAY NOT BE ANYWHERE NEAR what it was during the golden era, arcade gaming has never found a stronger foothold in modern culture than it has right now. For children of the 1970s and 1980s, these games bring back a special feeling that most modern games fail to capture. They crafted an experience around the act of playing the game. Most games of the day averaged less than a minute of actual playing time per quarter, but you'd bet you had been there for much longer than a minute. Another quarter, another minute; the cycle continued.

Despite uncertainty and unrest never feeling greater than it did at that moment, a group of innovators knew that there was something greater out there than pinball and coin-op paper card games . . . they just didn't know what it was. Yet through relentless trial and error, as became the manifesto at Atari, they pushed forward, risking everything they held dear to create entertainment for the masses centered on one thing: fun.

What they created formed the basis for video gaming as we know it today, cementing their position as industry pioneers while simultaneously inspiring the next generation.

For those who worked on the games, it was a challenge unlike anything experienced before or ever again. They learned as they went, but everything they did was but another stone on the pathway of gaming history. Not everything was a hit, and the company certainly wasn't perfect, but they were creating history, and history is rarely perfect.

For players, it was an inspiring time. There was something new and innovative around every turn. One day you were playing in black and white, the next you were playing in color. One day you were at an arcade, the next you were playing on the TV in your own home.

In twelve short years, Atari redefined entertainment, built that into a multibillion-dollar industry, and drove it straight back into the ground. While the effects of this last part should not be understated, the journey along the way resulted in the creation of a new art form, one that seeks to inspire and delight with each new game, just as Atari cofounder Nolan Bushnell had always intended. We were treated to everything from a simple game of virtual table tennis to the horrifying realities of nuclear war. It was a period of innovation that challenged what most believed to be possible, transforming modern life as we knew it. Without Atari, there most certainly would have been others who would find a way to commercialize Ralph Baer's vision, but without Nolan Bushnell, it most certainly would not have been as fun.

Rich Adam went on to program the arcade release of *Gravitar*, a vector-based space combat game. He left Atari in 1983, continuing to work in games for more than two decades. He now leads his own technology consulting firm.

Al Alcorn left Atari in 1981 following creative differences about the direction of the company. He wanted to move beyond the Video Computer System into other areas of innovation. Ray Kassar disagreed, and Alcorn eventually stopped showing up to work entirely. They called this "the beach" at Atari: you could retain your salary and benefits until the end of your contract, but were asked not to come in or do any work. It was an unofficial severance of sorts. Following his departure, he helped consult for tech startups and eventually joined Apple, leading the team that would develop the compression technology required to interpret video as a file format, MPEG. He continues to work in research and development to this day. He regrets telling Steve Jobs that Apple stock "wasn't worth using as wallpaper" when asked to invest.

Ralph Baer continued to create gaming consoles following Atari's dominance over the Magnavox Odyssey, helping both Coleco and Magnavox create competing home consoles. He later sued Atari for copyright infringement over the release of *Pong* and was awarded $700,000. He retired shortly thereafter. Though Nolan Bushnell initially tried to portray himself as the inventor of the video game, Baer is universally considered to be the "father of video games." He passed away on December 6, 2014, at the age of ninety-two.

After leaving Atari in 1978, **Nolan Bushnell** purchased back his original creation, a chain of pizza restaurants that featured arcade gaming and animatronics, which was then called Pizza Time Theatre; he eventually renamed it Chuck E. Cheese's Pizza Time Theatre. The company would later go bankrupt due to the video game crash of 1983, but it was revived by former rivals of Bushnell, and now has more than five hundred locations across the United States, fulfilling Bushnell's vision of a place that kids could enjoy arcade gaming in a family environment. Bushnell also created Catalyst Technologies, a business incubator focused on creating the products of the future, with Al Alcorn. He received a percentage of Atari's profits throughout the company's historic run. He is now focused on improving children's education.

Ted Dabney stayed in close touch with Nolan Bushnell after leaving Atari in 1973. He went on to help consult on Bushnell's Catalyst Technologies and Pizza Time Theatre while also working at Fujitsu and Radeon Semiconductor. Eventually he decided he wanted to leave the high-stress Silicon Valley life, and he moved to Crescent Mills, California, where he went on to own and operate a grocery store. Ted passed away on May 26, 2018 at age 81 from esophageal cancer.

Ray Kassar was cleared of all insider trading allegations against him and retired, becoming a private collector and investor. Though his work at Atari eventually ended in disaster, he saved the company's Video Computer System from discontinuation, popularized the home console, and grew Atari into a multibillion-dollar corporation. He passed away on December 10, 2017 in Vero Beach, Florida, at the age of eighty-nine.

Dave Theurer remained at Atari following the completion of *Tempest*, creating *I, Robot* (a commercial flop, now widely regarded as the first commercially produced video game to feature 3-D polygonal graphics and camera-control options) and *APB*. He left in 1990 to create an early game art tool, DeBabelizer, and now works as a programmer at a software management company. He was awarded the Pioneer Award at the 2012 Game Developers Conference for his work at Atari.

Walt Williams left 2K Games following the release of *Spec Ops: The Line*, eventually cowriting *Star Wars: Battlefront 2* at EA Motive, which was released in 2017.

Atari was sold to French software publisher Infogrames in 2000, and continued to grow as Infogrames purchased more of the company's stock over the course of the next decade. Though it appeared dead after declaring bankruptcy in 2013, the company has since reemerged as Atari, SA, with a focus on "new audiences."

Acknowledgments

THIS BOOK WAS A CHALLENGE. IT ISN'T AN EASY FEAT TO LOOK back nearly forty years, find information that's never been found before, and collect it in a coherent way—in fact, it's nearly impossible. I spent five years researching this book, digging through forum archives, newspaper articles, and interviewing people who never thought they would be interviewed about *Missile Command*. There were times it seemed like everything would come together perfectly and times it felt like it was foolish to believe it was ever going to happen in the first place; yet, somehow, we're here.

Thank you to my wonderful wife Sydnee for putting up with my endless late night writing sessions and ramblings about trackball settings. Your constant encouragement was invaluable. To my dad, Gary, for always believing in my wild video game dreams. Thank you to my saint of a literary agent, Eric Smith, without whom none of this would be possible. He took my proposal and fought through nearly all of publishing until he found the perfect person who wanted to help share our story. Adam O'Brien, my amazing editor and that perfect person, who took the project under his wing and helped push us through the finish line . . . even if we just barely made it in time. Huge thanks to Shelby Ozer and Chris Cappello at The Overlook Press for helping ensure that we did publicity and rights management just right, no matter how weird of requests I made.

Most importantly, I want to thank Dave Theurer, Nolan Bushnell, Rich Adam, Al Alcorn, Tony Temple, Rob Fulop, Phil Klemmer, and even Roy "Mr. Awesome" Shildt for entrusting me with this story. They were generous with their time, memories, and introductions. Without all of them, there wouldn't be a book and I'd still be wishing I had found a way to tell this amazing story.

Tim Lapetino and Blake J. Harris: without their advice and mentorship throughout this process, this book would be much, much worse. They helped both my writing and authorship develop in a way that has me light-years ahead of where I was when I began this journey. I can't thank them enough.

Finally, the book would not exist in one form or another without the additional help from the following people: Andrew Groen, Meggan Scavio, Ryan "Gootecks" Gutierrez, Harold Goldberg, Chris Melissinos, and Ryan Holiday.